Everything Oz

Quadrille
PUBLISHING

CONTENTS

COME JOIN US
and the
WONDERFUL WIZARD OF OZ

Welcome to *Everything OZ*, whether you are a mischievous Munchkin or a beautiful Good Witch, we hope you enjoy this journey down the Yellow Brick Road!

Following the success of our first book, *Everything Alice*, we are delighted to take *The Wonderful Wizard of OZ* as the theme of this follow-up book. Determined to do this much-loved tale justice, we have had fun gathering together ideas based on the original

book, as well as taking inspiration from the many stage and film adaptations.

After creating the projects and testing the recipes, the first part of the photoshoot took place in a London studio on possibly the hottest days of the year.

Hannah designed and built a set with a traveling show theme to fit the theatrical style of the late nineteenth century, when the original book was written.

We loved shooting the green-painted Emerald City Confectionery Cart (see page 85), which was adorned with delicious candy delights. The giant paper Field-O-Poppies (see pages 64–7) was so beautiful we didn't want to take it down. It took us a very late night to prepare them and, once dusted with a sprinkling of magical glitter, they seemed as though they were straight out of a movie.

Alongside photographer Verity, we risked working not only with an animal but also a child! We kept it in the family with Hannah's gorgeous nephew Christian, who modelled the supercute Little Monkey Baby's Bath Towel (see pages 112–15). The fabulous Maggie – aka Toto – is Hannah's

Chicken Catcher Verity

sister-in-law's Miniature Schnauzer, who showed off the stylish Best-in-Show Toto's Jacket (see pages 98–9) to perfection. Maggie was so well behaved, she could be a professional model!

Then it was off to East Sussex. The farm we shot at is just down the road from the home of Christine's parents. It has a very traditional Victorian feel to it and is full of chickens, pigs, and barking dogs. The resident peacock had a serious bee in his bonnet against Verity's car, which left with several scratches! We have to say a big thank you to the owners Mr & Mrs Peters.

At the farm we had planned to shoot outside, but that was when it rained… and rained… and rained. So lights were wrapped in plastic bags, rigged outside under umbrellas and shone

CHRISTINE SAYS …

I remember reading the Wizard of Oz curled up on my bed . The grey opening chapters didn't seem too promising at first but when the cyclone came and whisked Dorothy off to the Land of Oz, I went with her … Dorothy enthralled me, the Munchkins made me laugh, the Winged Monkeys frightened me and the whole book transported me to a wonderful world of make-believe.

A very wet Christine

✷ ✷ ✷ ✷ ✷ ✷ ✷ ✷ ✷ ✷ ✷ ✷

A BRIEF HISTORY OF OZ

✷ ✷ ✷ ✷ ✷ ✷ ✷ ✷ ✷ ✷ ✷ ✷

through the windows of outhouses to simulate daylight. Meanwhile, we were head-to-toe in waterproofs… all looking like three damp Dorothys!

Over the few days we were at the farm, thankfully the weather did improve and we got some fabulous outside shots such as the The No-Brainer Scarecrow (see pages 42–3). We made some little orange feathered friends along the way… well, Verity did. We were determined to get a hen in the photograph of Dorothy's Raffia Flower Basket (pages 44–6); hilariously, only Verity was confident enough to catch one, so she was nicknamed the Chicken Catcher!

Once all the shots were taken, it was time to head back to London. Christine set about designing the pages of the book and Hannah to create the illustrations. We can truly say we adore this book and hope you too are whisked away into a magical world of your own.

A love of the theatre is where this story begins. L. Frank Baum, author of *The Wonderful Wizard of OZ*, was infatuated by the stage.

Born in 1856 in Chittenango, New York, Baum was a kind man with a generous nature. With the help of his father, Baum founded a theatre in 1880 and set about writing plays. Sadly the theatre burnt to the ground, ironically while the show *Matches* was playing. Devastated by the loss of his scripts and costumes in the fire, Baum moved to South Dakota with his new wife. At the time the area was drought ridden; his later depiction of Kansas was based on this experience. He attempted many business ventures, several of which nearly bankrupted him. He ran Baum's Bazaar, but his generosity with credit led to the store's demise. Following these failures, Baum started to write down the nursery rhymes he improvised and told to his sons over the years. *Mother Goose in Prose* was published in 1897 to immediate success. In 1899 he collaborated with illustrator W.W. Denslow on *Father Goose: His Book* which met with rave reviews and became a bestseller.

The year 1900 saw the publication of another collaboration between Baum and Denslow, *The Wonderful Wizard of OZ*, which was met with great acclaim and adapted as a musical for Broadway in 1903. Baum met the demand for the first book by continuing a series of OZ stories.

A move to Hollywood and three more successful books followed in 1910, however in 1911 Baum was declared bankrupt. He began the OZ Film Manufacturing Company, experimenting with film effects, but the company folded after a year.

After years of failing health, Baum died in 1919. He is buried in the Forest Lawn Memorial Park Cemetery, Glendale, California.

CRAFT ESSENTIALS

★★★★★★★★★★★★★★★★★★★★★★★★★

A good craft kit is like a magpie's nest; full of little scraps of fabric, paper and sparkly things that may just be put to use one day.

Scissors: *Never mix up your scissors for cutting paper with your scissors for cutting fabric; they will stay sharper for longer if they do only one job. Small embroidery scissors are useful for snipping stray threads and pinking shears create decorative edges.*

Craft knife or scalpel

Wire cutters

Glue: *PVA glue is useful as an adhesive and a sealant. A glue-gun is great for fixing thing fast and specific glues for fabric, paper and superglue are also handy. Glue dots come in all shapes and sizes and are a clean and easy way to fix things.*

Tape: *Sellotape, invisible, masking and gaffa.*

Staple gun or stapler

Paper fasteners

Sewing machine

Sewing needles: *A good selection of needles with various size holes and thickness, including ones for embroidery. A big blunt needle with a large eye is very useful for threading ribbon or elastic through hems.*

Pins

Threads: *Various cotton and silk threads for sewing and embroidery.*

Tailor's chalk or a fading pen

Tape measure

Steel ruler

Assorted paint brushes

COOKERY ESSENTIALS

★ ★

*Good quality cookery utensils will not only last you
years but also help you achieve perfect results.*

Kitchen scales & measuring spoons
Wooden spoons
Measuring jug
Sieve
Whisk: *Electric, balloon or food processor.*
Rubber spatula: *Perfect for cleaning bowls.*
Rolling pin
Mixing bowls: *Big ones for cakes and small
ones for icing.*
Baking tray: *Best with edges, for extra grip
when removing from a hot oven.*
Cupcake or muffin tin

Foil, clingfilm & baking paper
Cooling rack
Jam thermometer
Cocktail sticks
Cupcake cases
Piping bags: *Disposable ones are best to
reduce mess.*
Piping ends: *A 1cm nozzle for macarons
and a selection of smaller star and writing
ends for decoration.*
Knives: *Bread knife and other sharp knives.*
Selection of cutlery

DRESS-UP DOROTHY & TOTO

with apron, basket & lion mask

✳ ✳

Dorothy, of course, is the star of the show and so needs a celebrity wardrobe! Accessorise this delightful doll with her very own gingham apron, straw basket and fancy-dress lion mask. Accompanied by her faithful companion, Toto, Dorothy is ready for any occasion.

YOU WILL NEED

For Dorothy

20cm x 30cm white cotton fabric
20cm x 40cm blue-and-white gingham cotton fabric
30cm x 30cm black-and-white striped cotton fabric
A4 sheet of brown wool felt
Scraps of wool felt in both white and red
Matching sewing threads
Medium-sized black, dark pink or red and pale pink colouring pens for face
Soft toy stuffing
Two small buttons

For Toto

A4 sheet of black wool felt
12cm x 12cm of 2cm-thick wadding
Matching sewing thread
15cm length of thin red ribbon

For the basket

A4 sheet of brown felt
Scraps of red and green felt
Matching sewing thread

✳ Using the templates on page 134, cut the following from the white fabric: one head and four arms. Cut the following from the gingham fabric: two bodies. Cut the following from the striped fabric: four front and back legs. Cut the following from the brown felt: one back head and one front hair. Cut the following from the red felt: four front and back shoes. Cut the following from the white felt: one front and back collar.

✳ To create Dorothy's face, simply lay the brown front hair over the white head to frame her face. Then draw her facial features onto the white cotton using the pens. We used black for her eyes and nose, then dark pink for her lips. Next, we dabbed dots of pale pink pen onto our fingers, which we then pressed onto the fabric to colour her cheeks (1). It is a good idea to draw Dorothy's face before you start sewing as it can sometimes go wrong; this way it is easy to replace this piece if you are dissatisfied with the results.

✳ Once you are happy with Dorothy's features, stitch the brown front hair around the drawn face. Top stitch approximately 5mm inside the edge of her hairline: if you are feeling adventurous, create some swirly locks of hair with extra lines of stitching.

✳ To make up the body, attach the front and back white felt collars to the two body pieces, then join. Hem the bottom edges of the body. Stitch the bottom edge of the head and the back of head to the correct body pieces, ensuring that the seam is facing inwards (2).

✳ To make up the legs, position one red felt shoe on the foot of each leg. Tack in place. Join the legs together in pairs with right sides facing, leaving the top edge open. Turn right sides out. Fill firmly with toy stuffing, packing evenly from the toes upwards using the round-ended handle of a wooden spoon (3).

join the arms

8

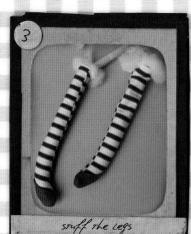

3

stuff the legs

5

9

Dorothy in her gingham apron

6

7

★ Make the arms in the same way as the legs. Position the arms, facing inwards, at the top of the body and tack in place (4).

★ Plait together three 15cm x 1cm lengths of brown felt, securing the ends with a few stitches. Repeat for the second plait. Position each plait, facing inwards, on the head and tack in place.

★ Place the joined head and body pieces together with right sides facing. Stitch all round the outside edges, leaving the hem of the dress open. Turn right side out, then stuff (5).

★ Position the legs inside the dress hem, curving inwards. Stitch to close the hem.

★ Add a button to the collar. Stitch the plaits into loops and add a red felt poppy.

TOTO

★ Fold the felt in half, sandwiching the wadding in between. Pin together.

★ Using the Toto template on page 127, trace the outline onto the felt. Sew zigzag stitches all round the outline. Trim the excess felt close to the line of stitches.

★ Tie a length of red ribbon into a bow around his neck.

BASKET

★ Using the template on page 127, cut the following from the brown felt: two basket sides. Also cut one 1.5cm x 17cm rectangle for the handle and one 5cm x 22cm rectangle for the base.

★ Join one long side of the base to one basket side, curving it around the bottom corners. Repeat for the second side. Turn right side out.

★ Position the ends of the handle centrally on opposite sides of the basket. Secure with reinforced stitching.

★ Place a rectangle of card in the base of the basket if it needs more structure.

★ Add a simple appliqué felt apple and leaves to one side of the basket.

LION MASK

YOU WILL NEED

A4 sheet of wool felt in each of yellow and orange
Scraps of cream and black wool felt
Matching sewing thread
Fabric glue

✻ Using the templates on page 127, cut the following from yellow felt: one head and two ears. Cut the following from orange felt: one mane and one head. Cut the following from cream felt: one muzzle. Cut the following from black felt: two eyes, one nose, one mouth and four whiskers.

✻ Position the muzzle on the yellow head. Secure with zigzag stitches. Using glue, add the eyes, nose, mouth and whiskers. Pinch the ears in the middle and pin to the edge of the head.

✻ Snip along the mane, where marked on the template. Position the mane in between the yellow and orange heads. Stitch all round the sides, securing the mane and ears in place, but leaving the bottom edge open.

GINGHAM APRON

YOU WILL NEED

50cm x 30cm blue-and-white gingham
30cm length of thin white lace
Matching sewing thread
Red embroidery thread

✻ Using the templates on page 127, cut one apron and one pocket from the gingham fabric. Also cut one 50cm x 5cm rectangle for the waistband and one 16cm x 4cm rectangle for the neckstrap.

✻ Turn under, press and topstitch a 1cm hem all round the apron. Fold both the waistband and neckstrap in half lengthways. Turn under and press a 1cm hem along the long edges. Stitch all the way round. Attach the ends of the neckstrap to the sides of the bib and the waistband centrally across the apron.

✻ Along the curved side of the pocket, clip notches into the seam allowance. Turn under, press and topstitch a 1cm hem all round. Position the pocket on the apron skirt, pin and work neat blanket stitches in red embroidery thread around the curve.

✻ Trim the neck edge and the hem of the apron with lengths of white lace.

Aunt Em's
FRENCH CRULLERS

✫ ✫

Kansas is a mighty fine place to try French-influenced desserts. Aunt Em's family recipe has been passed down through generations; consider yourself lucky she has shared it here!

YOU WILL NEED

235ml full-fat milk
120ml water
115g caster sugar
½ teaspoon salt
115g unsalted butter
230g self-raising flour
Few drops of vanilla extract
4 large eggs, beaten

For the glaze
230g icing sugar, sieved
2 tablespoons maple syrup
2 tablespoons milk

You will also need a piping bag fitted with a 1cm star nozzle

✳ Preheat the oven to 200°C/gas mark 6.

✳ Cut two pieces of baking parchment to the size of your baking sheets. Using a 10cm diameter mug, draw six pencil circles onto each piece of parchment, spacing them about 3cm apart. Turn over the parchment so the pencil marks are on the underside. Place on the baking sheets.

✳ Pour the milk and water into a deep saucepan. Add the sugar, salt and butter and place over a medium heat. Stir continuously with a wooden spoon until the butter has melted. Turn up the heat and bring the mixture to the boil. Add the vanilla extract.

✳ Add the flour all at once. Continue stirring briskly with a wooden spoon until the mixture forms a ball and leaves the sides of the pan clean. Beat vigorously for 1–2 minutes before removing from the heat. Transfer to a ceramic or glass bowl and leave to cool for 5 minutes.

✳ Add the eggs one at a time, beating with a wooden spoon. Once the eggs is incorporated, the paste will be thick and glossy.

✳ Spoon the mixture into a piping bag fitted with a 1cm star nozzle. Using the pencil marks as a guide, pipe equal rounds onto the baking parchment.

✳ Bake for 15 minutes. Reduce the oven temperature to 190°C/gas mark 5 and bake for a further 20 minutes or until the pastries are golden brown. The crullers will really puff up, almost doubling in size. Once baked, place on a wire rack to cool.

For the glaze
✳ Place the icing sugar, maple syrup and milk together in a bowl. Mix until thick, glossy and there are no lumps.

✳ Slide a piece of baking parchment underneath the wire rack. Brush or spoon the glaze over the crullers (1). Sprinkle with a little more icing sugar before serving.

brush or spoon over the glaze

Faithful Friend

TOTO
CUSHION

✷ ✷

"IT WAS TOTO THAT
MADE DOROTHY LAUGH,
AND SAVED HER FROM
GROWING AS GREY AS
HER SURROUNDINGS."

~ Chapter 1 ~
The Cyclone

This ultra-soft cushion puts to good use any old sweaters you may have lying around. Woollens with a cashmere content are super snuggly.

YOU WILL NEED

Two 70cm x 50cm rectangles of white fabric for lining
70cm x 50cm woollen fabric, such as an old sweater or cardigan, for outer cover
Matching sewing thread
Tailor's chalk or air erasable fabric pen
Soft toy stuffing
Two 2cm circles of black or brown wool felt for eyes
Gingham scarf, cloth or napkin for bow

Note: If you are using an old sweater, cut away the neck and arms only to create rectangles of fabric. Do not cut down the sides of the sweater. Leaving the seams intact makes it easier to keep everything in place when sewing the cushion together.

By making two cushions – one from lining fabric and one from a stretchy woollen fabric – you get a better shape dog.

✷ Fold the white lining fabric in half lengthways, with right sides facing, and pin together. Using the template on page 128, trace the outline onto the fabric. Machine stitch around the outline, leaving a 10cm turning hole along the dog's underbelly. Trim the excess fabric close to the line of stitching (1).

✷ Make notches in the seam allowance of the fabric along the curves around the ears, nose, tail and legs (2). This will give a better overall shape and neater curves.

✷ Turn the lining right side out. Using the handle of a wooden spoon, open out all the curves, such as the tip of the tail. Press.

✷ Repeat the previous steps but this time using the woollen outer cover fabric. As the woollen fabric will be quite stretchy, stitch slightly inside the outline to avoid a mis-shapen Toto (3).

✷ Turn the outer cover right side out and carefully insert the shaped lining. Make sure the ears, nose, tail and legs are all aligned and lay flat.

✷ Firmly fill the cushion with toy stuffing, pushing it into all the extremities. Close both of the openings with neat hand stitches.

✷ Add a small circle of black or brown felt to either side of the head for eyes.

✷ Finally smarten up Toto by tying a gingham scarf, cloth or napkin into a pretty bow around his neck.

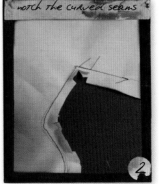

notch the curved seams

Uncle Henry's Famous
CHERRY PIE

✴ ✴

For a time it was illegal to serve ice cream with cherry pie in Kansas.
This recipe is so good, it is practically criminal!

YOU WILL NEED

For the pastry
300g plain flour
2 tablespoons icing sugar
Large pinch of salt
170g unsalted butter, chilled
170g cream cheese
60–80ml single cream

For the filling
1.3kg unpitted sweet cherries (or 1kg if pitted)
Juice of half small lemon
140g caster sugar
1 heaped teaspoon ground cinnamon
3 rounded tablespoons cornflour

You will also need a 23cm round pie dish

To make the pastry

✴ Sift the flour, icing sugar and salt together into a bowl.

✴ Cut the chilled butter into small dice and add to the flour with the cream cheese. Using your fingertips, rub the butter into the flour until it resembles coarse breadcrumbs.

✴ Pour in the cream a little at a time until the mixture forms a soft dough. Gather the dough into a ball and knead briefly to smooth out any lumps.

✴ Divide the dough equally into two and chill for at least 1 hour or overnight.

damn fine cherry pie

To make the cherry filling

✴ If unpitted, remove the stones from the cherries. Sprinkle over the lemon juice, caster sugar, cinnamon and cornflour. Gently combine until all the cherries are covered in the syrup. Leave to stand for at least 20 minutes, then stir once more.

✴ On a floured surface, roll out half the dough and use to line a 23cm pie dish or shallow tart tin. Roll out the remaining dough to a 23cm circle for the pie lid and place on a sheet of baking parchment. Chill both the pastry-lined pie dish and the lid until ready to bake.

✴ Preheat the oven to 220°C/gas mark 7.

✴ Pile the cherries into the pastry-lined pie dish to form a gently swelling mound. Brush the edges of the pastry case with water, then lay the lid on top. Crimp the edges firmly together with the tines of a fork. Trim any excess pastry. Cut a hole or holes in the pie lid to allow steam to escape. You can also add decorative pastry shapes to the lid using any excess dough.

✴ Bake for 20 minutes. Reduce the oven temperature to 180°C/gas mark 4 and bake for a further 30–40 minutes or until the cherry juice bubbles up through the steam holes. If the pastry is darkening too quickly, cover loosely with aluminium foil.

✴ Serve the cherry pie warm in slices with vanilla ice cream.

Over the Rainbow
FRILL CURTAIN

★ ★

This girly drape looks just as stunning in a bedroom or living room as it does in a barn. The delicate hues of each frill can be made more or less subtle to suit a variety of décors.

★ Measure the height of the window the frill curtain will be hung at. Using this measurement, hem the ready-made curtain accordingly to create the required drop.

★ To calculate the amounts needed of each coloured fabric, multiply the width of the ready-made curtain by 2.5 and add 3cm. This gives you your first measurement. Next, divide the length of the ready-made curtain by 7 and add 8cm. This give your your second measurement. The additional 8cm allows for both a 5cm overlap of each frill and the hem allowances.

★ Turn under, press and topstitch a 1.5cm hem on all sides of the seven pieces of cotton.

★ With an air-erasable fabric pen and metal ruler, lightly mark a guideline for where each coloured frill will be stitched onto the ready-made curtain. This helps to maintain a straight line when sewing. Do not forget that each frill should overhang the one below it by 5cm.

fold and pin the box pleats

★ Lay out the ready-made curtain on a clean floor. Beginning at the top edge, position the first frill along its sewing guideline and pin into a series of box pleats. We made five box pleats across the width of each of our frills. To make a box pleat, fold the fabric so that the two upper folds of the pleat face in opposite directions, while the two under folds are laid toward each other (1). Stitch the frill in place along the guideline.

★ Repeat for all the subsequent frills until the last one is in place and covers the bottom edge of the ready-made curtain.

★ Trim any loose threads, press and hang.

BLUEBIRD WREATH

✴ ✴

Somewhere over the rainbow, bluebirds fly! What could be more joyful than this chirpy all-seasons wreath. The brightly wool-wrapped ring brings a sparkle to a wall or door.

YOU WILL NEED

35cm polystyrene half-ring wreath
Three balls wool yarn in different colours
Hot-glue gun
Selection of brightly coloured felt for flowers
Selection of trims
Decorative bluebirds

Note: For inside use only, as wet weather may cause damage or colour to run

✴ With the ends to the back, wrap the yarn closely around the polystyrene wreath (1). Vary the thicknesses of each section. The thicker the yarn, the less time this stage takes.

✴ To create decorative flowers, cut out six petal shapes from felt. Dot a blob of glue on one end of each petal and pinch into shape (2). Join them all together using a hot-glue gun, then add a button or gem to the centre.

✴ Vary the petal shapes to create different flowers. Arrange all your felt flowers, along with any other trims, around the wreath. Once you find your preferred arrangement, hot-glue gun them in place on the wreath.

✴ Finally, hot-glue gun your bluebirds to the wreath, nestled in the felt flowers.

Dorothy's PATCHWORK APRON

✶ ✶

This patchwork apron is great for using up all your rainbow coloured scraps of fabric.

YOU WILL NEED

65cm x 55cm plain coloured cotton fabric for apron front
65cm x 55cm print cotton fabric for apron back
Remanant of various print fabrics in different colours, each large enough to make a 10cm wide rectangle for pocket front and tie
65cm x 25cm plain coloured cotton fabric for pocket back
Tailor's chalk
Matching sewing thread
Embroidery thread

To make the apron

✶ Place the plain cotton apron front together with the print cotton apron back with right sides facing. Pin together and fold in half widthways. With tailor's chalk, mark the points 30cm down from the from the top edge and 20cm in from the side. Draw and cut a gentle curve between these two marks through all the fabric layers (1).

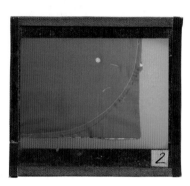

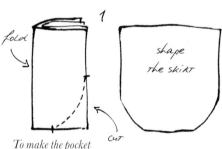

To make the pocket

✶ Cut 10cm wide rectangles of varying lengths – but no longer than 25cm – from different print fabrics. Stitch these together with a 1cm seam allowance to create a patchwork piece that is about 65cm x 25cm.

✶ Place the patchwork pocket piece together with the plain cotton pocket back with right sides facing. Stitch all the way round leaving a small turning hole along the base of the rectangle. Turn right side out and press.

✶ With the plain front on top and the print back below, place the pocket between these two layers of fabric aligning bottom edges. Make sure the plain pocket back is face up and the edge with the turning hole is at the

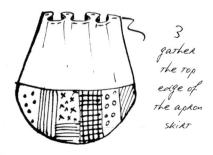

bottom. The square corners of the pocket piece will extend beyond the curved edges of the apron skirt. Pin all the layers together (2).

✶ Starting at one top corner and following the curved lines, stitch down the side and around the apron skirt up to the opposite corner leaving the top edge open. Trim the corners of the pocket piece into curves. Turn right side out and press. To create divisions in the pocket, stitch along a few of the vertical seams of the patchwork.

✶ Using a length of embroidery thread, sew a line of loose running stitch along the top edge. Gently gather the fabric to a width of 42cm and secure the thread at either side (3).

To make the tie

✳ The tie of this apron wraps around the waist and makes a bow at the front: it is 3m long. If you prefer a tie that does up at the back, shorten it to 2m.

✳ Cut about thirty 10cm wide rectangles of varying lengths – but no longer than 30cm and no shorter than 10cm – from different print fabrics. Divide the rectangles in two equal piles with a similar amount of long and short pieces. This is to ensure the front and back of the tie is the same length.

✳ Cut four 15cm wide rectangles that are 20cm in length from different print fabrics. This is to ensure the end sections of the tie are slightly wider than the rest.

✳ Using one of the piles, join two rectangles together along the short edge. Repeat this until all the rectangles are joined in pairs. Next, join two pairs of rectangles together along one short edge. Repeat this until all your rectangles are joined together to create one long tie. As you sew, check the length of the tie by wrapping it round your waist. Once it reaches your preferred length, join a set of 15cm-wide rectangles to each end of the tie. Repeat with the second pile of rectangles, matching the length to the first tie.

✳ Press each tie piece and place together with right sides facing. Fold in half to find the mid-point of the tie. Measure and mark the points 22cm either side of the mid-point. This is where the apron skirt will be inserted.

tie a bow

✳ Starting at a marked point and working outwards, stitch all the way round to the second marked point. Gradually widen the tie at the ends and stitch a diagonal rather than vertical line up the short sides. Turn right side out and press. Turn under and press a neat hem along the opening.

✳ Insert the top of the apron to the opening of the tie, spreading the gathers evenly across the width. Pin and topstitch the tie opening closed and the apron skirt into place.

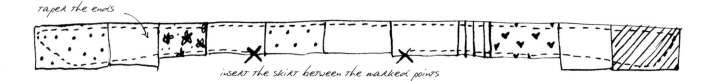

taper the ends

insert the skirt between the marked points

LAST EDITION

The Kansas Daily Tribune.

VOLUME XXXVII   WICHITA, KANSAS JUNE 4. 1890   TUESDAY MORNING

WINDSWEPT!
GIRL TAKEN BY CYCLONE

DOROTHY GALE RETURNS FROM GREAT TWISTER ADVENTURE

Speaking exclusively to The Kansas Daily Tribune on her return, Dorothy Gale tells of her experiences RIGHT AT THE HEART OF THE CYCLONE!

"Well, the house whirled around two or three times and rose slowly through the air. I felt as if I were going up in a balloon."

In a freak of nature the north and south winds met where the house stood, and made it the exact center of the cyclone. According to experts in the middle of a cyclone the air is generally still, but the great pressure of the wind on every side of the house raised it up higher and higher, until it was at the very top of the cyclone; and there it remained and was carried miles and miles away as easily as you could carry a feather.

"It was very dark, and the wind howled horribly around me," Dorothy continues, "but I found I was riding quite easily. After the first few whirls around, and one other time when the house tipped badly,

I felt as if I were being rocked gently, like a baby in a cradle."

TOTO'S FEARS

"Toto did not like it. He ran about the room, now here, now there, barking loudly; but I sat quite still on the floor and waited to see what would happen."

"Once Toto got too near the open trap door, and fell in; and at first I thought I had lost him. But soon I saw one of his ears sticking up through the hole, Experts tell me the strong pressure of the air was keeping him up so that he could not fall. I crept to the hole, caught Toto by the ear, and dragged him into the room again, afterward closing the trap door so that no more accidents could happen."

ALL ALONE

"Hour after hour passed away, and slowly I got over my fright; but I felt quite lonely, and the wind shrieked so loudly all about me that I nearly became deaf. At first I had wondered if I would be dashed to pieces when the house fell again; but as the hours passed and nothing

terrible happened, I stopped worrying and resolved to wait calmly and see what the future would bring. At last I crawled over the swaying floor to my bed, and lay down upon it; and Toto followed and lay down beside me."

"In spite of the swaying of the house and the wailing of the wind, I soon closed my eyes and fell fast asleep."

HOME SWEET HOME

Dorothy declines to comment on what happened after this but she does say, "This trip has taught me there is no place like home."

CYCLONE CUPCAKES

Get swept away by these luscious lemon cupcakes with a mini-meringue tornado topping.

YOU WILL NEED

for the sponge cupcakes

100g unsalted butter, softened
100g caster sugar
Zest of 1 lemon, finely grated
2 eggs, lightly beaten
100g self-raising flour, sifted
¼ teaspoon baking powder

for the filling

Jar of lemon curd

for the meringue topping

2 egg whites
125g caster sugar

makes 12 cupcakes

To make the sponge cupcakes

✳ Preheat the oven to 180°C/gas mark 4. Line a 12-hole muffin tin with paper cases.

✳ Place the butter, sugar and grated lemon zest in a bowl and, using either a wooden spoon or an electric mixer, cream together until light and fluffy.

✳ Add the beaten egg gradually, mixing well after each addition.

✳ Once all the egg has been incorporated into the butter mixture, fold in the sifted flour and baking powder and stir until just combined. This will ensure the sponges stay light and fluffy.

✳ Bake in the oven for 15–20 minutes, depending on your oven. After 10 minutes, check the sponge by inserting a wooden cocktail stick into the middle. If it comes out clean, they are cooked. If it comes out covered in crumbs, bake for a further few minutes. To avoid the sponge drying out, do not overcook at this stage as they will go back in the oven later.

To make the meringue
Even the smallest speck of grease or fat in the egg whites or on the bowl or utensils can affect how stiffly egg whites whip up. Make sure you separate

the eggs carefully, use a super-clean whisk and a glass or metal bowl. Eggs that are a couple of days old used at room temperature create stiffer peaks.

✳ Using an electric whisk set on medium, whisk the egg whites until stiff peaks form in the bowl. (A hand balloon whisk is fine too, it just takes longer and is much more tiring.)

✳ Gradually add the sugar to the egg whites, whisking constantly until the mixture turns glossy with silky consistency. The meringue is ready when the peaks hold their shape rather than flop over… or when you can hold the bowl upside down over your head and nothing falls out!

To decorate the cupcakes
✳ Place a small teaspoon of lemon curd in the centre of each cupcake.

✳ Transfer the meringue mixture into a piping bag fitted with a round nozzle. Pipe meringue whirlwinds on top of each cake, completely covering the lemon curd.

✳ Return to the oven for approximately 10 minutes or until the meringue is golden brown and firm to the touch.

✳ Leave on a wire rack to cool. Eat the cupcakes within two days.

SQUASHED WITCH CUPCAKES

✶ ✶

Take a leaf out of Dorothy's book and be sure to squash all the bad witches. The difference with these Squashed Witch Cupcakes is they leave a totally delicious taste in your mouth!

YOU WILL NEED

for the sponge cupcakes

125g self-raising flour
½ teaspoon baking powder
½ teaspoon baking soda
50g unsweetened cocoa powder
½ teaspoon salt
30g unsalted butter, softened
225g caster sugar
1 egg, lightly beaten
Few drops of vanilla extract
180ml full-fat milk

for the decoration

Small amounts of white, black, green and red readymade icing
Wooden skewer
Edible red glitter
Icing sugar for dusting
Cake glue or egg white
Apricot jam

makes 12 cupcakes

To make the sponge cupcakes

✶ Preheat oven to 175°C/gas mark 4. Line a 12-hole cupcake tin with foil cases.

✶ Sieve the flour, baking powder and soda, cocoa and salt together in a bowl. Place the butter and sugar in a separate bowl and cream together until light and fluffy. Add the vanilla extract. Add the beaten egg gradually, mixing well after each addition.

✶ Once the egg has been incorporated, fold in the sifted dry ingredients a few spoonfuls at a time, alternating with the milk.

✶ Fill the cases three-quarters full only with the sponge mixture. Bake for 15–18 minutes or until a wooden toothpick inserted in the middle comes out clean. Leave to cool on a wire rack then store in an airtight container.

To decorate

✶ For each leg, roll out an 8cm length of white icing about 6mm thick. Repeat with the black icing, but roll it to half the thickness. To create the stripes lay one end of the black icing on the white at an angle and then roll, pressing lightly as you go (1).

✶ For each shoe, roll out a 2cm ball of red icing, then flatten it slightly. Make a small divot where the leg inserts into the shoe and then form the other end into a point for the toe. Using cake glue or egg white, fix a striped leg to each shoe. Shape the shoe's heel using a wooden skewer (2). Sprinkle over edible red glitter (3). Leave the legs and shoes to harden overnight.

✶ Lightly dust a work surface with icing sugar. Roll out the green icing to a thickness of 3mm. Using a round serrated cookie cutter slightly wider that the tops of the cupcakes, press out twelve green skirts.

✶ To assemble, for each cake place a small circle of baking parchment on your serving plate and sit a pair of legs on top. Brush a thin layer of apricot jam on the tops of the legs and lay a green skirt over the legs. Brush another layer of jam over the skirt, place an upside-down cupcake on top and gently press.

Wicked Witch of the East's RUBY SLIPPERS

✴ ✴

There's no place like home! Transform old heels into a magical pair of Ruby Slippers. Using easy elasticised trim, create shoes with minimum mess and maximum durability.

YOU WILL NEED

Pair of heeled shoes, cleaned
Bright red or metallic silver spray paint
Old newspaper
Hot-glue gun
4m of red or silver elasticated sequin trim, 2.5cm-wide

✴ In a well-ventilated space (preferably outdoors), spray paint the shoes either red or silver. Use sheets of old newspaper to protect surfaces from the paint. There is no need to paint the insides or soles. Leave to air dry.

✴ Beginning at the back of the shoe, just above the heel, attach one end of the elasticated sequin trim to the upper using the hot-glue gun (1). Working around the bottom edge of the shoe, glueing as you go, completely cover the shoe's upper with rows of the sequin trim (2).

✴ Once the upper is fully covered, wrap the shoe's heel in the sequin trim beginning at the bottom and working up to the top.

✴ To make a bow, cut a 20cm length of sequin trim. Fold both ends inwards and fix in the middle with glue to create two bow loops. Cut a shorter 6cm length of sequin trim and wrap it around the middle of the bow to cover the centre join. Fix a bow to the front of each sequin-covered shoe using the hot-glue gun. Allow the glue to dry fully.

✴ Slip on your sequin shoes, click your heels together and see where you end up!

"Dorothy said, with hesitation… "I have not killed anything." "Your house did, anyway," replied the little old woman, with a laugh, "and that is the same thing. See!" She continued, pointing to the corner of the house. "There are her two feet, still sticking out from under a block of wood." Dorothy looked and gave a little cry of fright. There indeed, just under the corner of the great beam the house rested on, two feet were sticking out, shod in silver shoes with pointed toes."

~ Chapter 2 ~
The Council with the Munchkins

GLINDA PEG DOLL

✦ ✦

Create your very own glamorous Good Witch from a simple wooden clothes peg

YOU WILL NEED

Old-fashioned 'dolly'
wooden clothes peg
15cm length of thick
garden wire
Hot-glue gun
Red and black felt-tip pens
for face
20cm x 12cm pink cotton
fabric
10cm x 15cm silver tuille
with glitter dots
Two 6cm x 15cm white
tuille
Pink embroidery thread
Thin orange yarn for hair
Silver card for crown
Three silver star gems
One round silver gem
6cm length of thin silver
wire for wand

✦ To make the basic frame and arms, loop the thick garden wire around the 'body' of the clothes peg, just above the split. Add a dot of glue at the back to hold the wire in place.

✦ To create Glinda's face, draw her features onto the 'head' of the peg using the pens. It is best to draw the face now as it can go wrong; it is easier to replace the clothes peg now if you are dissatisfied with the results.

✦ To make the underskirt, fold the pink fabric in half widthways. With the folded edge at her feet, fix one end of the fabric in place with a line of glue just under the wire arms. Wrap the fabric around the body and fix the other end neatly at the back with a line of glue on the overlapping sides (1).

✦ Lay the piece of silver tuille over the pink fabric. Make small pleats in the tuille as you wrap it around. Fix in place by again applying a line of glue around the top edge.

✦ To cover the arms, add a dot of glue to the end of the left-hand wire. Attach one end of the pink embroidery thread to the wire and wrap to form a small ball. Continue wrapping the wire all the way up the arm until you reach the body. Carry the thread over to the right-hand arm and repeat; finish with a dot of glue and a small ball at the end (2). To cover the bodice, wrap the body diagonally in both directions until covered.

✦ To make the hair, glue one end of the orange yarn to the back of the head. Wrap around the head neatly until covered. Finish with a dot of glue to the back of the head (3).

✦ To make the sleeves, fold the pieces of white tuille in half lengthwise. Pinch the ends together and glue. Place over the arms and glue on the underside to secure. Glue the round gem to the front of her bodice.

✦ Using the template on page 129, cut a crown from silver card. Glue the ends together, add a star gem to the front and place on her head. To make the wand, sandwich the thin wire between two star gems. Glue in place to one of her hands.

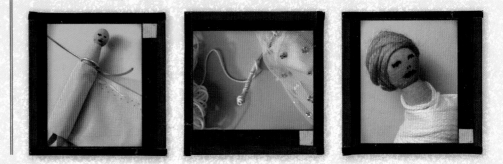

MUNCHKIN HAT EGG COSIES

"The Munchkins wore round hats that rose to a small point a foot above their heads."
These decorated felt hats are equally cosy for heads and eggs alike!

YOU WILL NEED

Selection of wool felt
squares in various colours
(we used three shades of
blue, two shades of green,
two shades of yellow, pink
and red)
A selection of embroidery
threads in contrasting
colours
Embroidery needle
Scissors or pinking shears
Selection of small felt
pompoms, buttons,
sequins and bells in
various colours for
decoration

To make the hat cosy
✳ Using the template on page 129, cut one
hat from coloured felt. Using the same
template, cut one brim from a contrasting
shade of felt. Place the brim in position on
top of the hat and join the two pieces along
the base using blanket stitch (1).

✳ With the brim on the inside, fold the hat
in half widthwise. Join the edges from
bottom to top using blanket stitch. Turn
about 2cm of the brim to the right side.
This creates the basic hat.

To make the feather and flower decoration
✳ Using the templates on page 129, cut out
different size feathers from coloured felt and
one flower centre in a contrasting shade. For
a crimped edge, use pinking shears to cut out
the shapes. Lay the smaller feathers on top of
the larger ones and fix in place with a line of
running stitch. Tuck the tip of the feathers
into the brim of the hat, then place the flower
centre on top and stitch in place. Add a few
coloured sequins to the centre for decoration.

✳ Using the templates on page 129, cut two
flower petals from coloured felt; cut one
centre and one leaf in contrasting shades.
Place one petal shape on top of the other to
form a cross. Pinch together in the middle
and fix with a few stitches. Add the centre
and leaf, then decorate with a bell or button.

> 1 — work a line of blanket stitch

> 2 — decorate with feathers

MUNCHKIN
PLACECARDS

✴ ✴

We all know the Munchkins host a great party,
so why not let them guide your guests to their seats.

YOU WILL NEED

2 sheets of A4 scrapbook
paper in different patterns
Spray glue
10cm x 5cm of white card
Black and pink felt-tip pens
For a girl munchkin:
10cm x 10cm scrapbook
paper in a contrasting
pattern for apron
For a boy munchkin:
10cm x 2cm glitter card
for waistband
Flower shapes punched
from card (optional)
Small felt pompoms
Two 15cm lengths of thin
silver wire
PVA glue
Stapler
Hot-glue gun

Makes 2 placecards

✴ Using spray glue, fix together the sheets of
scrapbook paper so the patterned sides are
face out. Using the templates on page 129,
cut one body from the double-sided paper
and cut one face from the white card. Using
felt-tip pens draw features on to the white
card face; it's fun to mimic the features of
your guests (1).

✴ Glue the face in place on the body. Using
a black felt-tip pen, add further details to the
body, such as a collar, hair and buttons on the
hat. Using the templates on page 129, cut one
apron for a girl or one waistband for a boy
from a contrasting pattern. Glue in place on
the body. Add a felt pompom to the hat and a
punched paper flower to the apron (2).

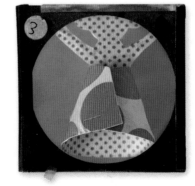

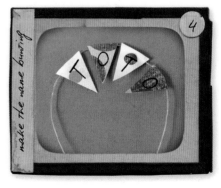

✴ Shape the skirt of the body into a cone by
bending the corners back until they overlap
by 1cm. Hold in place with a staple (3).

✴ Cut a paper triangle for each letter, write
on the letters then attach to the wire using a
hot-glue gun (4). Bend and cut the wire to
size. Glue each end to the back of a hand.

Baum's Bazaar
❧ BOX-O-BRICKS ❧
COCONUT ICE

★★★★★★★★★★★★★★★★★★★★★★★★★★★★★★★★★

This Yellow Brick Road Coconut Ice recipe will have you addicted to eating bricks!

YOU WILL NEED

350g dessicated coconut
350g icing sugar, sieved,
plus extra for dusting
100g condensed milk,
plus extra
Few drops of vanilla extract
Brown and yellow food
colouring

✳ Place the dessicated coconut and icing sugar together in a large mixing bowl. Add the condensed milk, a splash at a time, and combine until the mixture forms a dough but is not too wet.

✳ Place one-fifth of this mixture in a separate bowl and add a few drops of brown food colouring. To the other four-fifths of the mixture add yellow food colouring to create a vibrant shade.

✳ Lay three lengths of baking parchment on your worksurface and dust with icing sugar. Divide the yellow mixture into two halves. Place one half on a length of parchment and, using a rolling pin, roll out to a thickness of about 1cm, keeping the shape as square as possible. Repeat with the second half, then roll out the brown mixture to a thickness of about 3mm.

✳ Place the brown square, parchment side up, on top of one of the yellow squares. Using a rolling pin, lightly press down on the layers so they stick together, then peel away the parchment. Repeat with the remaining yellow square to create a sandwich with the brown layer in the middle. Take care when rolling not to flatten the layers of the block too much.

✳ Wrap the block in parchment, slide onto a baking sheet and chill in the fridge to harden. Using a sharp knife, cut the block into individual brick shapes measuring 4cm by 2cm. For perfectly straight lines, use a metal ruler to cut the bricks.

"The road to the City of Emeralds is paved with yellow brick," said the Witch, "so you cannot miss it."

~ Chapter 2 ~
The Council with the Munchkins

The *No-brainer* SCARECROW

✲ ✲

Create your own super-cute scarecrow. What he may lack in scariness, he makes up for in homespun charm!

YOU WILL NEED

Two bamboo canes, one shorter than the other, for the arms (adjust the length of the canes according to how tall you want your scarecrow to be)
Brown garden twine
Waterproof toy stuffing or straw for head and body
Brown parcel tape
40cm x 40cm hessian or similar rough brown fabric
1m print cotton fabric for body
20cm x 20cm white cotton fabric for collar
Three self-cover buttons
Matching sewing thread
Ball of yarn for hair

✲ To make the frame, form a cross with the bamboo canes with the horizontal cane for the 'arms' positioned about 20cm from the top of the vertical cane. Make sure both arms are of equal length. Tie the canes together firmly using brown garden twine.

cover the head

✲ To make the 'head', form the toy stuffing or straw into a ball. Tape this ball to the top of the vertical cane. Don't worry if this looks messy as it will be covered in the next stage. Lay the head on one corner of the brown hessian fabric (1). Fold the other corners of the fabric over so it covers the head and tie securely around the neck with twine.

✲ Using the template from page 130 scaled to suit the size of your scarecrow, cut two body pieces from the print cotton fabric. Embroider a trouser fly outline onto one

body piece using blue thread. Cut one collar from the white cotton fabric and stitch to the same body piece at the neck edge.

✲ Place the body pieces together, with right sides facing. Join, leaving the bottom edge open. Turn right side out. Place over the canes, sliding the horizontal cane from side to side.

✲ Tuck the hessian into the body and stitch around the neck edge. Fill with toy stuffing or straw then close the bottom edge with blanket stitch (2). Cover the buttons with print cotton following the manufacturer's instructions and sew to the front of the body.

✲ To make the hair, tightly wrap a 20cm x 3cm scrap of print cotton fabric wrap around the ball of yarn and stitch in place on the top of the head. To finish, embroider or paint the scarecrow's face on the front of the head.

RAFFIA FLOWER BASKET

"DO LET ME CARRY
THAT BASKET FOR YOU.
I SHALL NOT MIND IT,
FOR I CAN'T GET TIRED,"
SAID THE SCARECROW

~ Chapter 3 ~
How Dorothy Saved the Scarecrow

★ ★

Customise a basket bag with these great lining and raffia flower techniques.

YOU WILL NEED

for the basket lining

Lining fabric (to calculate how much you need, measure the basket following the instructions)
Tape measure
Matching sewing thread

for the decoration

Lengths of raffia in two different colours
Flower loom
Tapestry needle
Hot-glue gun
Selection of wool felt in various colours

To make the basket lining

★ First, measure the basket. To find the length of the side panels, measure from 6cm below the outside rim of the basket to the inside base. To find the width of the side panels, measure along the inside of one short and one long side of the basket. Measure the width and length of the inside of the basket's base. Add 3cm to all measurements for the seam allowances.

attaching the lining base

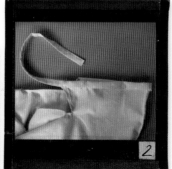

★ Following these measurements, cut two side panels and one base panel from the lining fabric. Measure the position of the handles in relation to the rim. Transfer these measurements onto the side panels.

★ Allowing for 1.5cm hems, cut triangular flaps at the marked points on the side panels to accommodate the handles. Turn under 1.5cm hems around these openings, notch the allowances and topstitch.

★ Place the two side panels together, with right sides facing. Stitch with 1.5cm seam allowances to form a tube. Pin the base panel to the sides, with right sides facing (1). Stitch with a 1.5cm seam allowance, notching the seam if necessary.

★ To make the ties, measure the outer rim of the basket. Divide this measurement in half and then add 40cm. Cut two 3cm-wide strips of lining fabric to this length. Fold the strips in half lengthwise, with right sides facing, and press. Stitch along all sides.

★ Turn under and press a 1.5cm hem all the way round the top edge of the lining. Leaving the end 20cm free, pin and then stitch the ties along the top edge, beginning and ending at the handle openings (2).

★ Place the lining inside the basket and turn the overhanging lining down over the rim to the outer side of the basket. Knot the ties into decorative bows just below the handles.

RAFFIA FLOWERS

This retro 1970s technique is a great way to vamp up any boring old bags, hats or purses.

✶ Separate a length of raffia in your chosen colour and tie a knot in it about 10cm from one end. Thread the raffia through the hole at the edge of the flower loom. Check it is secure.

✶ Wind the raffia backwards and forwards over opposite pegs, travelling around the loom. You may need to join additional lengths of raffia onto the original length; to do this simply tie the two ends into a neat knot and trim any excess. Once the raffia has been wound around all the pegs, trim the loose end to about 10cm and knot to first end.

✶ Thread a tapestry needle with a different colour raffia. Bring the needle up from the underside between the loops of one petal and then pass it back through the centre of the flower. Repeat this until all the petals have been sewn.

✶ Once all the petals have been secured, carefully remove the raffia flower from the loom. Make as many raffia flowers in various sizes and colours as preferred.

✶ Using a hot-glue gun, attach the raffia flowers to the side of your basket. We also added extra felt flowers (see the instructions on page 22) and leaves, as well as pearl bead and bell trims.

Baum's Bazaar

DOROTHY
❧ GIFT TAGS ☙

for perfect presents and gorgeous gifts

.1.
COLOUR PHOTOCOPY
THE GIFT TAGS
ONTO THIN CARD

.2.
CUT OUT THE GIFT
TAGS AND PUNCH
HOLES FOR THE
RIBBON TIES

.3.
THREAD THE TAGS
WITH RIBBON
AND WRITE YOUR
MESSAGE ON
THE REVERSE

The Scarecrow's
BRAN NEW BRAINS
MUFFINS

* *

*We all know the most important meal of the day is breakfast, so don't be a silly Scarecrow,
why not have one of these delicious energy-fuelled treats to keep your brains at their best!*

YOU WILL NEED

115g salted butter, room
temperature
100g brown sugar
2 bananas, mashed
115ml milk
1 teaspoon of vanilla extract
2 large eggs, lightly beaten
130g wholemeal flour
100g wheat bran
1 teaspoon baking powder
1 teaspoon baking soda
½ teaspoon salt
75g chunky mixed nuts and
granola breakfast cereal, plus
extra for topping

Makes 16 muffins

* Preheat the oven to 190°C/gas mark 5.
Line a 6-hole or 12-hole muffin tin with
paper cases following the instructions given
below for Tulip Muffin Cases.

* Place the butter and sugar in a bowl and
cream together until light and fluffy.

* Add the mashed bananas, milk, vanilla
extract and beaten eggs. Stir through until
the ingredients are fully combined.

* In a separate bowl, combine the
wholemeal flour, wheat bran, baking
powder and soda and salt. Add the banana
mixture. Once the ingredients are evenly
mixed, gently stir in the breakfast cereal.

* Spoon the mixture into the tulip muffin
cases and bake for 15 minutes. Remove
from the oven and sprinkle with some
extra cereal. Return to the oven and bake
for a further 5–10 minutes, or until a
wooden skewer inserted into the middle of
the muffins comes out clean.

* Leave to cool slightly in the muffin tin
but serve while still warm, if you can.

make the muffin cases

TULIP
MUFFIN
CASES

YOU WILL NEED

Muffin tin
Unbleached baking
parchment
Paper drinks cup
Brown parcel string (optional)

* Cut the baking parchment into 15cm
squares, one for each muffin case required.

* Lay each square centrally over a muffin-
tin hole and, using a paper drinks cup, push
the paper down into the hole to form a tulip
shape. With your nails, score along the folds
to define the natural creases in the paper.

* Add the muffin mixture to the cases and
bake in the tin. Often the cases hold their
shape better when doubled up.

* Once the muffins are cool, tie with a little
brown string bow for a more rustic finish.

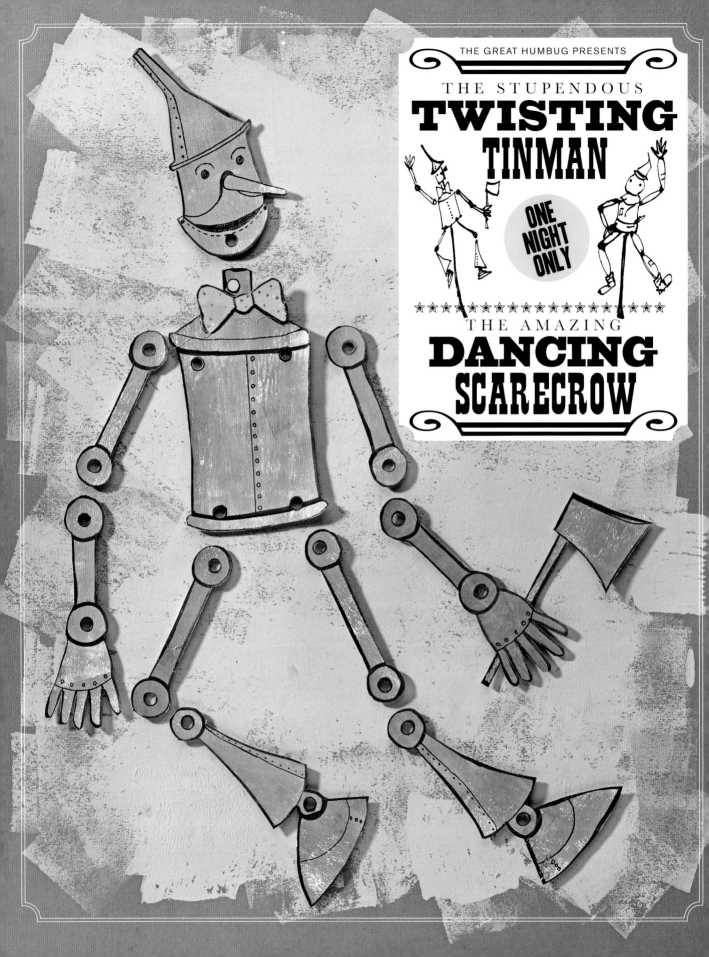

THE GREAT HUMBUG PRESENTS

THE STUPENDOUS
TWISTING
TINMAN

ONE
NIGHT
ONLY

THE AMAZING
DANCING
SCARECROW

.1.
COLOUR PHOTOCOPY
THE PUPPET ONTO
THIN CARD.

.2.
CUT OUT ALL THE
PARTS AND PUNCH
HOLES FOR THE PINS.
JOIN THE PARTS
USING SPLIT PINS.

.3.
ADD A HANDLE BY
GLUEING A WOODEN
SKEWER TO THE
CENTRE BACK.

.4.
SPIN THE HANDLE
BETWEEN YOUR
PALMS AND WATCH
THEM DANCE.

The Tin Woodman's HEART GARLAND

✶✶✶✶✶✶✶✶✶✶✶✶✶✶✶✶✶✶✶✶✶✶✶✶✶✶✶

All the Tin Woodman wanted was a heart, and with this garland he can have one for every day of the week.

✶ Photocopy or trace the templates on page 131. Cut out each shape. Using a sharp pencil, draw around each paper template onto the tin sheets. For our garland, we made two large, three medium and two small hearts plus two birds and two wings.

✶ Wearing protective gloves, cut out the shapes with the tin snips or scissors.

✶ Decide on your design for the decoration and draw it onto the tin shapes with a pencil. Place the first heart onto the wooden block then, using a small tin punch and hammer, tap out the design. Experiment with different size punches: for example, a flat-head screwdriver gives a rectangular shape. Also, the harder you hammer, the deeper the impression.

"MY HEAD IS QUITE EMPTY," ANSWERED THE WOODMAN: "BUT ONCE I HAD BRAINS, AND A HEART ALSO; SO, HAVING TRIED THEM BOTH, I SHOULD MUCH RATHER HAVE A HEART."

~ Chapter 5 ~
The Rescue of the Tin Woodman

✶ To remove any sharp edges, dampen the wet-and-dry paper and rub all over the metal shapes in a circular motion. This burnishes the tin and makes the hammered pattern stand out.

✶ Drill hanging holes in the hearts and two larger holes at points A and B on the birds' backs. Use the wooden block for drilling.

✶ To make the garland, cut three 2m lengths of natural garden twine and plait together. Knot each end, leaving about 20cm unplaited.

✶ Thread a tin bird onto each end of the plaited garland. Using strong adhesive, glue the bird's wing in place so it covers the string and any holes. Glue a small button on top of the wing.

✶ To hang each heart, cut a 20cm length of twine and fold in two. Thread both ends through the tin heart until only a small loop is left. Thread the two cut ends of twine through the loop. Repeat with the remaining hearts.

✶ Finally, hang the hearts, evenly spaced and according to size, along the plaited garland in your preferred order.

TIN CAN LANTERNS

✮ ✮

Set the mood with these delectable tea light holders.

YOU WILL NEED

Selection of tin cans, emptied, cleaned and labels removed
Marker pen
Acrylic or spray paint in a selection of bright colours
Wooden block (small enough to fit inside the empty cans)
Electric drill
Dustpan and brush

Caution: Never leave a lighted candle unattended.

✮ Check the tin cans are thoroughly clean; there must be no residues of food on the inside or glue from the label on the outside.

✮ Decide on your designs for the decoration and draw it onto the outside of the cans with a marker pen.

✮ Paint the inside of the cans with a bright colour. (Vibrant shades look great when illuminated by the candlelight.) Allow the paint to dry completely.

✮ Place the wooden block inside the can; this makes it easier and safer when drilling the design. (If you don't have a wooden block, fill the can with water and freeze it.)

✮ Following the guidelines, drill small holes in the cans to create the decorative pattern. Once the design is complete, brush away any tin residue and check for sharp edges.

✮ Place a lighted tea light inside each tin can lantern.

"I SHALL TAKE THE HEART," RETURNED THE WOODMAN, "FOR BRAINS DO NOT MAKE ONE HAPPY, AND HAPPINESS IS THE BEST THING IN THE WORLD."

~ Chapter 5 ~
The Rescue of the Tin Woodman

The Tin Woodman's
CHOCOLATE-OIL
SILVER-NUT SUNDAE

This delicious warm chocolate sauce will keep your elbow joints moving…
moving the spoon from the glass to your mouth!

YOU WILL NEED

For the chocolate sauce
100g plain chocolate
(minimum 70% cocoa
solids)
397g can sweetened
condensed milk
2 tablespoons butter
1 teaspoon vanilla extract

For the silver nuts
Few handfuls of mixed
nuts, such as almonds,
hazelnuts and walnuts
Edible silver paint spray

For the sundae
Tub of good-quality vanilla
ice cream
Edible silver stars and
chocolate stars for
decoration
Indoor sparklers (optional)

Makes 4 sundaes

For the chocolate sauce
✳ Break the chocolate into chunks and place half of it into a heavy based saucepan.

✳ Add the condensed milk and butter then place over a medium heat. Stir continuously until the chocolate has melted – do not allow the mixture to boil.

✳ Check the sauce and – if you want an even more chocolately taste – add more squares of chocolate. (This isn't strictly necessary as you can simply add all the chocolate at the beginning… but any excuse to try the sauce!)

✳ Remove the sauce from the heat and stir in the vanilla extract.

For the silver nuts
✳ Place the mixed nuts in a dry frying pan and toast for a couple of minutes over a high heat. Leave to cool.

✳ Once cool, spray the nuts with edible silver paint spray. Allow to dry completely.

To assemble the sundae
✳ Place a few of the silver nuts in the bottom of a sundae glass. Pour over a glug of the warm chocolate sauce then add a scoop of vanilla ice cream. Repeat this to create another layer. Top the sundae with two round scoops of vanilla ice cream then drizzle over some more warm chocolate sauce. Decorate with a few more silver nuts, a chocolate star and a sprinkle of edible silver stars.

The Cowardly Lion
HAND PUPPET

"WHAT MAKES YOU A COWARD?" ASKED DOROTHY, LOOKING AT THE GREAT BEAST IN WONDER, FOR HE WAS AS BIG AS A SMALL HORSE.

~ Chapter 6 ~
The Cowardly Lion

This little lion with his shivering quivering mane isn't scared of a thing, no Siree, not him, no way… "Ooh, what was that?"

YOU WILL NEED

Four A4 sheets of yellow wool felt for face and body
A4 sheet of orange wool felt for mane
A4 sheet of cream wool felt for muzzle
A4 sheet of pink wool felt for ears, nose and mouth
Various scraps of print fabrics for tummy and mane, maximum size 40cm x 20cm
Embroidery thread in each of the following colours: yellow, orange, pink and black
Two black buttons, about 1cm–1.5cm, for eyes
Scissors
Felt flower in a contrasting colour (optional)

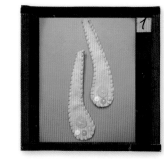

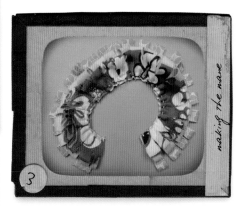

✶ Using the templates on pages 132–33, cut all the required pieces from coloured felt and print fabric. Sew the tummy onto the front body. Add the paw detail to two of the arms and sew then together in pairs (1).

✶ Sew the pink inner ears to the orange outer ears then position the ears either side of the face and tack in place (2).

✶ For the mane, cut three rectangles – one 40cm x 10cm from orange felt, one 40cm x 8cm and one 40cm x 14cm from print fabrics. Fold each rectangle in half lengthways and place in a stack with the felt in the middle. Join the layers along the raw edges with running stitches then slightly gather. Make 3cm snips into each layer of the mane at 2cm intervals along the folded edge (3). Position the mane around the top the back and tack in place. Place the face on top and stitch (4).

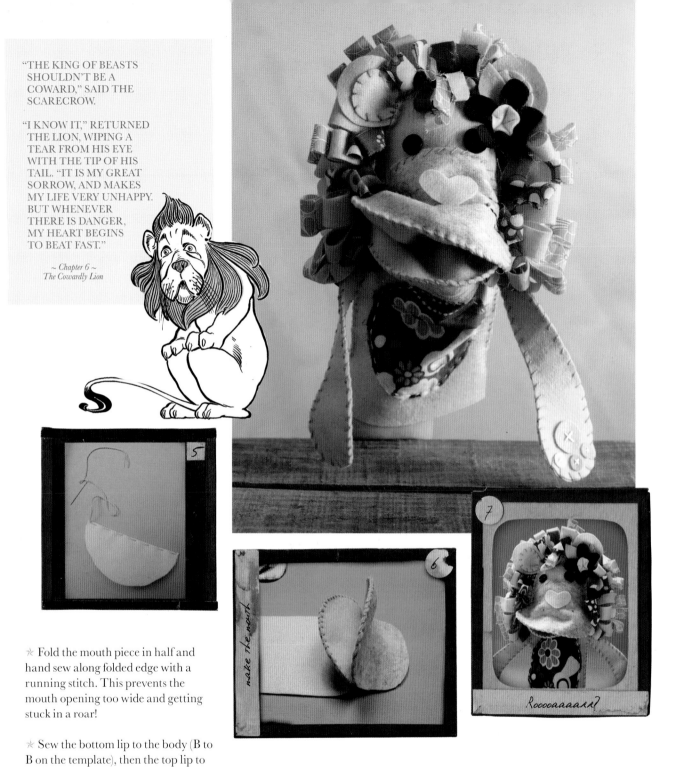

"THE KING OF BEASTS SHOULDN'T BE A COWARD," SAID THE SCARECROW.

"I KNOW IT," RETURNED THE LION, WIPING A TEAR FROM HIS EYE WITH THE TIP OF HIS TAIL. "IT IS MY GREAT SORROW, AND MAKES MY LIFE VERY UNHAPPY. BUT WHENEVER THERE IS DANGER, MY HEART BEGINS TO BEAT FAST."

~ Chapter 6 ~
The Cowardly Lion

make the mouth

Rooooaaaarr?

✶ Fold the mouth piece in half and hand sew along folded edge with a running stitch. This prevents the mouth opening too wide and getting stuck in a roar!

✶ Sew the bottom lip to the body (B to B on the template), then the top lip to the nose (A to A on the template).

✶ Lay the body on top of the back and line up the nose with the face (C to C), overlapping the felt by about 1cm. (The body will be longer than the back at the base of the puppet.)

✶ Stitch the nose to the face and embroider on some whiskers. Attach the eyes. You can use buttons, felt shapes, beads or teddy bear eyes.

✶ Start sewing each side of the body together inserting the arms between the body pieces about 5cm down from the mouth.

✶ Make a small fringe using the same fabric as the mane, stitch in place in between the ears. Decorate with a felt flower or rosette.

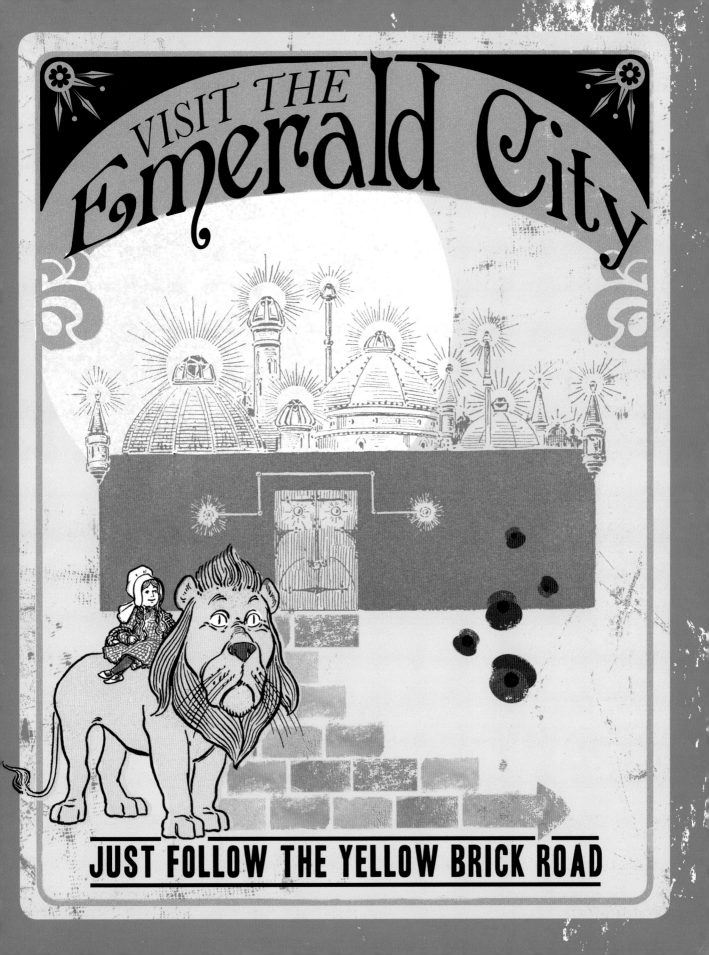

GIANT ROSETTES

awarded for **COURAGE**

"THAT DOESN'T MAKE ME
ANY BRAVER, AND AS LONG
AS I KNOW MYSELF TO BE A
COWARD I SHALL BE UNHAPPY."

~ Chapter 6 ~
The Cowardly Lion

★ ★

Sometimes decorating a party can seem daunting, but take courage! Why not take a leaf out of the Lion's book by creating these stunningly simple rosettes.

YOU WILL NEED

Three A1 sheets of paper in contrasting colours for rosettes
Two A4 sheets of patterned scrapbook paper for rosette centre and ribbons
Thin silver wire
Stapler
Glue
Length of ribbon for hanging

★ First, decide on your colour scheme and ther order in which they will be placed. The entire width of an A1 sheet of paper is used for the base rosette ring, then different coloured rings are added to build the design.

★ Lay the three A1 sheets of paper together, one on the top of the other, and concertina fold them into a fan shape by folding backwards and forwards in 6cm widths. Use the edge of a metal ruler to make crisp folds.

concertina the papers together

★ Once the papers are fully folded, open out the concertina and separate the sheets. Trim both ends of each sheet into a gently curved petal shape.

★ Cut the second sheet about 10cm shorter either side than the first, so the middle rosette ring will have space around it. Repeat for the third sheet but 20cm shorter.

★ Layer the sheets together again, matchingthe folds exactly and making sure the smallest pieces is centrally placed (1).

★ With the papers lined up, fold the fan in half to find the centre point. Wrap the wire around the centre point in a loop, tightly securing the sheets. Open out the rosette and staple each end together to join.

★ From patterned scrapbook paper, cut a circle to your preferred size and glue to the centre of the rosette. Add two paper ribbon lengths, glued to the reverse of the rosette.

★ Attach a length of ribbon to the wired centre and hang at your desired location.

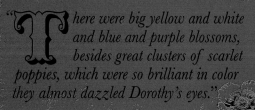

"There were big yellow and white and blue and purple blossoms, besides great clusters of scarlet poppies, which were so brilliant in color they almost dazzled Dorothy's eyes."

~ Chapter 8 ~
The Deadly Poppy Field

FIELD ~O~ POPPIES

These stunning giant flowers look fantastic in bunches and can be made to any size.
They are great to use big as party decorations, or make in a smaller display for a table.

YOU WILL NEED

A1 sheet of red card
A3 sheet of black and leaf
green card
1m bamboo cane
Green spray paint (same
colour as leaf green card)
Gaffer tape
Red glitter

concertina fold the petals

shape the 3D petals

✳ Using the templates on page 134, for each poppy cut out five petals from red card, two stamen from black card and two leaves from green card.

✳ Concertina fold the petals lengthways about three-quarters of the way up. Make sure the centre fold is in line with the slit and is a valley fold, in other words it folds inwards (1).

✳ Flatten the petal folds out slightly. To make the petal 3D, overlap the base of the petal where there is a slit. Staple in place (2). Repeat for all the petals.

✳ Staple three 3D petals together in a rough triangle, with two close together and the third slighty on its own (3).

making the poppy

4

★ Then staple the remaining two petals either side of the single petal (4).

5

create the stamen

★ To create the stamens, fold where marked on pattern and glue one to the other in the middle, make sure the stamens stalks alternate. Glue this to the middle of the poppy and gently curl the ends using a closed pair of scissors or your fingers (5).

6

the finished flower

★ Glue the stamen into the centre of the poppy. Then fold each petal out and curl at the top (6).

★ Spray paint your bamboo cane green and allow to dry. Score the leaves down the middle and with hot-glue gun fix them to the cane.

★ Attach the poppy head to the stem using strips of gaffer tape. Cut four strips and stick first three along the underside of the flower down onto the bamboo cane, then the final one wrap around the others to secure. Try to do this as neatly as possible.

★ For a magical finish, sprinkle with red glitter sleepy dust.

Raggedy Patchwork
POPPY T-SHIRT

★ ★

Be truly en vogue with this beautiful poppy embellished t-shirt, a great way to customise clothes that need a new lease of life.

50cm x 50cm pieces of between three and five different red print cotton fabrics
Red embroidery thread

★ Cut sets of four circles all the same size from the different fabrics (1). To vary the flower sizes, cut some sets in varying sizes from one another, making some very small whilst others are oversized.

★ Lay the circles on top of one another and fold in half, then into quarters (2). Pinching the tip, stitch across the bottom edges to secure the shape (3). Repeat for as many poppies as you require.

★ Lay the poppies on your t-shirt before you attach them and pin into place. Once happy with the design, stitch neatly from below at the point of the flower and either side of the bottom petal layer (4).

pinch the petals together

sew onto the t-shirt

SLEEPY~TIME
EYEMASK

✶ ✶

When you're in need of forty winks, this embroidered eyemask will help you drift off into a field of dreams.

YOU WILL NEED

50cm x 50cm pale blue silk fabric, for eyemask front
Air erasable fabric pen
Embroidery hoop at least 25cm in diameter
Embroidery silks in various colours, including metallics
Fine embroidery needle
25cm x 25cm mid blue silk fabric, for eyemask back
25cm x 25cm soft fabric, such as velour or flannelette, for padding
50cm x 5cm pale blue silk fabric, for eyemask strap
30cm length of 5mm-wide elastic (adjust the length of the elastic to suit your head size)
Thin midnight blue ribbon (optional)

To stitch the embroidery

✶ Using the guide on page 135, trace the design on to the centre of the pale blue silk with an air erasable fabric pen. It is easier to see the lines if you hold the fabric up against a window. Mount the silk in an embroidery hoop, making sure the fabric is taut. Using two strands of embroidery silk and a fine needle, embroider the poppies by working small neat stitches over the guidelines (1).

To make the eyemask front

✶ Remove the embroidery from the hoop and lightly press. Using the template on page 135, trace the outline of the eyemask on to the silk, making sure the poppies sit across the centre. Lay the embroidered silk right side up on top of the padding. Pin the layers together then stitch all the way round, 1cm outside the outline (3). Cut out the eyemask front close to this stitch line.

To make the strap

✶ Fold the 50 x 5cm piece of pale blue silk in half lengthwise. Stitch down the longest edge, about 1.5cm in from the fold. As silk frays, keep a wider than normal seam allowance. Turn right side out and press with the seam in the centre of one side of this tube. Thread the elastic through the tube and fix to one end of the strap, securing it with a few stitches. Gather the silk tube evenly along its length and secure the other end of the elastic to the strap, again with a few stitches.

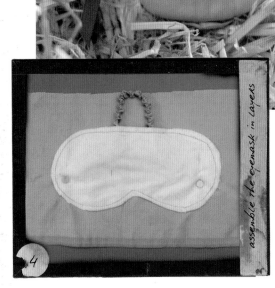

* Pin the layers together. Leaving a 5–6cm opening along the upper straight edge and avoiding the strap, stitch all the way round the eyemask following the template line.

* Trim the seam allowance back to about 6mm; it's fine to trim away the first stitch line from the eyemask front. Around the curves, snip small notches from the seam allowance to allow the fabric to stretch. Turn the eyemask right side out through the opening. The strap will fall in to place at the back of the eyemask. Gently ease the curves into shape and lightly press. Close the opening with small neat hand stitches. Tie short lengths of midnight blue ribbon in to neat bows at each end of the strap, if preferred.

* Tack the elasticated strap to the embroidered eyemask front at points "A" and "B". Place together the eyemask front and the mid blue silk with right sides facing. Arrange the strap so that it is contained within the shape of the eyemask front except the centre section, which should be visible at the top of the eyemask (4).

"They now came upon more and more of the big scarlet poppies, and fewer and fewer of the other flowers; and soon they found themselves in the midst of a great meadow of poppies. Now it is well known that when there are many of these flowers together their odor is so powerful that anyone who breathes it falls asleep, and if the sleeper is not carried away from the scent of the flowers, he sleeps on and on forever. But Dorothy did not know this, nor could she get away from the bright red flowers that were everywhere about; so presently her eyes grew heavy and she felt she must sit down to rest and to sleep."

~ Chapter 8 ~
The Deadly Poppy Field

OVER THE RAINBOW CAKE

✷ ✷

This cake is the perfect centrepiece to any party; make this for someone's birthday and take great delight in seeing the surprise on their face when they cut the first slice!

YOU WILL NEED

For the cake
350g unsalted butter, at
room temperature
350g caster sugar
5 large egg whites
3 teaspoons vanilla extract
350g self-raising flour
3 teaspoons baking powder
200ml milk
Violet, blue, green, yellow,
orange and red natural
food colouring

For the frosting
400g full-fat cream cheese
100g unsalted butter, at
room temperature
250g icing sugar
2 teaspoons lemon flavouring

For the decoration
Jelly diamonds

You will also need:
A selection of mixing bowls
One or more round 20cm
cake tins
Wire cooling rack
Cake card
Turn table
Plastic side-scraper
or palette knife

Serves 8–12 slices

To make the cake
✷ Preheat the oven to 180°C/gas mark 4. Line the cake tins with baking parchment.

✷ Place the butter and sugar into a large bowl and cream together until light and fluffy. Whisk the egg whites into the butter, one by one. Add the vanilla extract.

✷ In a separate bowl, sift together the flour and baking powder. Gradually add the flour to the butter, stirring only until the batter is just combined. Finally add the milk.

✷ Divide the batter equally between six bowls for the different coloured cake layers, with each sixth weighing about 250g. Add a few drops of one of the natural food colours to each bowl, blending the colour evenly.

✷ Spoon one of the coloured cake batters into a prepared cake tin and bake for 10–12 minutes, or until the top of the cake springs back to the touch. Ideally, use two or more cake tins and bake several layers together at the same time. Allow the cakes to cool fully before assembling and adding the frosting.

To make the frosting
✷ Place the cream cheese and butter in a bowl; blend until smooth. Sift in the icing sugar and add the lemon flavouring.

To assemble the cake
✷ Place a cake card on top of a turn table. Lay the violet coloured base cake layer on a

sheet of baking parchment and place on the turn table. Spread a thin coating of frosting evenly over the cake layer, then place the blue coloured cake on top. Repeat for each layer until the final red coloured cake.

✷ To crumb coat the layered cake, spoon a generous amount of frosting onto the top of the cake (1). Using a side-scraper, spread it evenly across the top and down the sides, turning the table against the direction of the side-scraper. Chill the cake for at least 30 minutes or until the frosting has set.

✷ For the final coat of frosting, repeat the previous stage with the remaining clean frosting. To finish, decorate the top of the cake with multi-coloured jelly diamonds.

assemble the cake in layers

"They all started upon the Journey, greatly enjoying the walk through the soft, fresh grass; and it was not long before they reached the road of yellow brick and turned again towards the Emerald City where the great OZ dwelt."

~ Chapter 10 ~
The Guardian of the Gates

PATCHWORK PICNIC SET

✶ ✶

Padded sitters are ideal for picnics as everyone gets their own comfortable seat, so there are no rows over who has the most blanket. They even have a waterproof base for damp days.

YOU WILL NEED

For each sitter:
22cm x 22cm plain cotton, for centre square
Selection of patchwork cottons in various prints, maximum 50cm x 30cm
Fusible bonding web
Matching sewing threads
Thick cardboard and ruler
Patchwork rotatary cutter and cutting mat
50cm x 50cm white lining fabric
35cm x 6cm each of oilcloth and patchwork cotton, for handle
50cm x 50cm oilcloth, for backing
48cm x 48cm wadding, 2cm thick

For the tablecloth:
61cm x 31cm print cotton, in three different colours
91cm x 31cm print cotton, in two different colours
29cm x 21cm lightweight cotton in four different colours, for 'placemats'
10cm x 10cm lightweight cotton in four different prints, for 'coasters'
122cm x 92cm cotton sheeting for backing

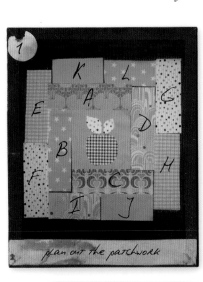

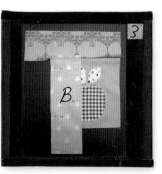

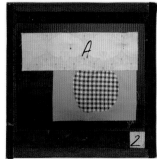

To make a sitter

✶ Using the templates on page 136, trace a reversed outline of the apple, heart, dog or house motifs onto the paper side of the fusible bonding web. Cut it out roughly and, with the adhesive side downwards, iron to the wrong side of the chosen print fabric. Next, trim precisely around the traced outline, peel away the paper and place the appliqué motif centrally on the plain centre square. Press the motif with a hot iron to fuse the adhesive.

✶ Secure the raw edges of the motif with either neat hand stitches or zigzag machine stitches in a coloured thread.

✶ Measure and cut three rectangular templates from thick cardboard, one in each of the following sizes: 9cm x 30cm (pieces A–D), 9cm x 28cm (pieces E–H), 9cm x 20cm (pieces I–L).

★ Select which prints are to be used for the patchwork rectangles, then press the fabric to remove any creases. Using the three cardboard templates, cut four rectangles of each size. For perfectly straight edges, use a patchwork rotary cutter and cutting mat.

★ Lay out all your patchwork pieces and make a record of the plan (1). You will need to refer back to this plan as you join the patchwork pieces.

★ With right sides facing, place patchwork piece A and the centre square together with raw edges aligning along the top edge. Machine stitch leaving a seam allowance of 1cm; stop at the edge of the centre square, leaving about 8cm of the rectangle unstitched (2). Repeat with the remaining three pieces B, C and D. When joining piece D, stitch along the entire length of the rectangle thereby joining it to the short side of piece A (5).

★ Go back around the square and join the three unstitched ends of the rectangles to the short ends of the adjacent pieces. Press open all the seams so they lie flat. Check the outside edges of the resulting patchwork square are straight and, if any of them are a bit wonky, trim them square (6).

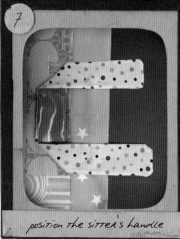

position the sitter's handle

★ Join pieces E and F along one short edge. Repeat with G and H, I and J, K and L. Press all the seams open.

★ Join the strip made from pieces I/J to the bottom edge of the patchwork square, aligning the seam of the strip with the middle of the centre square. Repeat at the top edge with the strip made from pieces K/L.

★ Join the longer strips made from pieces E/F and G/H to the left and right edges, again aligning the seams with the middle of the centre square. Press open all the seams so they lie flat. Check the outside edges of the final patchwork square are straight and, as before, trim if necessary.

★ With right sides facing, place the finished patchwork square and lining together. Leaving a 10cm opening along one edge, stitch all the way round leaving a 5mm seam allowance.

To make a handle
★ With right sides facing, place oilcloth and cotton handle pieces together. Leaving an opening at one end, stitch all the way round to form a tube. Turn right side out and press. Fold the handle into a 'C' shape and position centrally at the top edge of the patchwork square with the handle facing inwards (7). Pin in place.

★ With right sides facing, place the patchwork and oilcloth squares together. (The handle will be sandwiched between the two layers.) Starting at the bottom edge and leaving a 10cm opening, stitch all the way round. Turn right side out and press.

★ Feed the square of wadding through the opening, pushing into the corners

and flattening it out. If necessary, trim the wadding for a snug fit.

★ Close the opening with small, neat hand stitches. You have now completed one sitter. So have a little sit down… or make a few more.

To make the tablecloth
★ With one 61cm x 31cm rectangle as the centre panel, join the four other patchwork pieces to this panel in the same way as given for the sitters. Press open all the seams so they lie flat.

★ Position the 'placemats' and 'coasters' on the patchwork cloth and stitch in place. Add appliqué motifs if preferred.

★ With right sides facing, place the patchwork cloth and backing fabric together. Leaving a 20cm opening along one edge, stitch all the way round.

★ Turn the cloth right side out and press. Close the opening with small, neat hand stitches.

WELCOME TO THE EMERALD CITY

"BEFORE THEM STOOD A LITTLE MAN ABOUT THE SAME SIZE AS THE MUNCHKINS. HE WAS CLOTHED ALL IN GREEN...

WHEN HE SAW DOROTHY AND HER COMPANIONS THE MAN ASKED, "WHAT DO YOU WISH IN THE EMERALD CITY?" "WE CAME HERE TO SEE THE GREAT OZ," SAID DOROTHY. THE MAN WAS SO SURPRISED AT THIS ANSWER THAT HE SAT DOWN TO THINK IT OVER."

~ Chapter 10 ~
The Guardian of the Gates

GLOW-IN-THE-DARK EMERALD CITY JELLY

Dazzle your party guests with this marvellous jelly display and they will turn green with envy!

YOU WILL NEED Tonic water with quinine ★ Lime jelly mix
UV light ★ Selection of plastic sandcastle moulds

★ To make the jelly,
follow the instructions from the
green jelly packet, but in the final stage add the
tonic water instead of water.

★ Using clean dry sandcastle moulds you can form cityscapes.
If they are odd shapes and will not stand alone in the fridge, use a
bowl and pad out with some kitchen roll to keep the mould flat. Pour
your jelly liquid into the moulds and allow to set in the fridge. The
quinine in the jelly picks up UV light and appears to glow; it also
gives a distinctive bitter taste, which goes well with the lime jelly.

★ Turn out your set jelly on a plate and turn down the
lights, hold up your UV light to show of the
Emerald City glow!

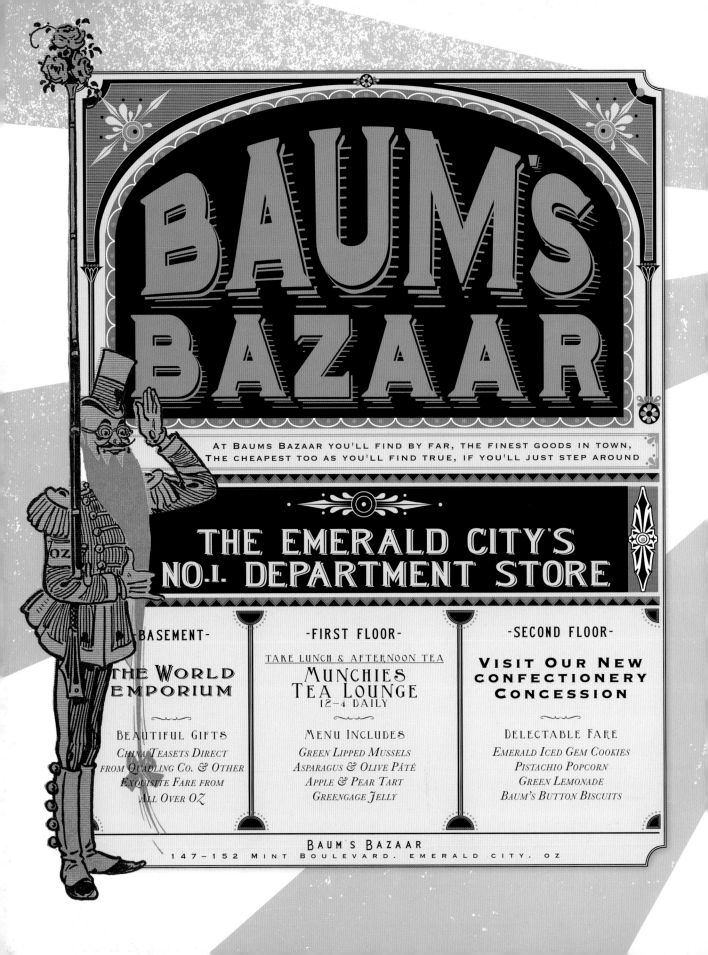

Baum's Bazaar
ICED GEM
❧ COOKIES ❧

These old favourites are a bestseller on the OZ Candy Cart. As soon as they're in stock, they sell out!

YOU WILL NEED

115g butter, softened
135g caster sugar
1 egg, lightly beaten
2–3 drops vanilla extract
210g plain flour
¼ teaspoon baking powder
¼ teaspoon salt

for the icing
300g royal icing sugar
Green food colouring
Green edible glitter

Makes about 30 cookies

✶ Place the butter and sugar into a large bowl and cream together until light and fluffy. Add the beaten egg and the vanilla extract.

✶ In a separate bowl, sift together the flour, baking powder and salt. Gradually add the flour to the butter to form a dough.

✶ Wrap the dough in clingfilm and chill in the fridge for at least 1 hour, but it can be left overnight.

✶ When ready to bake, preheat the oven to 200°C/gas mark 6.

✶ Place the dough on a floured surface. Roll out the dough to an even thickness of about 5mm. Using a 5cm round serrated cookie cutter, press out the shapes. Place on ungreased baking sheets about 2cm apart.

✶ Bake for 6–10 minutes until the cookies are golden brown at the edges. Allow to cool completely on a wire rack before icing.

For the icing
✶ Sift the icing sugar into a medium-sized bowl. Add a few drops of green food colouring and blend. Slowly add a little water – a drop at a time – to create a thick paste consistency.

✶ With a 1cm-wide star nozzle, pipe the icing onto the centres of the cookies. For extra sparkly gems, sprinkle with green edible glitter.

◈❀ **PISTACHIO POPCORN** ❀◈

The citizens of OZ favour this delicious salty-sweet popcorn, but it is a little too spicy for the sugary-toothed Munchkins.

YOU WILL NEED

200g pistachios, roasted, salted
and shelled
100g plain popcorn
2 tbsp unsalted butter
50g maple syrup
½ teaspoon curry powder
Green food colouring

☆ Pile the pistachios in the centre of a clean tea towel and gather up the edges. Using a rolling pin, smash the pistachios into small pieces. Place the nuts in a large bowl and add the popcorn.

☆ Melt the butter in a small saucepan over a low heat. Add the maple syrup and curry powder, then simmer for 3 minutes. Add a few drops of food colouring and mix. Remove from the heat, pour the butter over the nuts and popcorn, then stir to coat.

☆ Allow to cool before serving or storing in an airtight container.

Baum's Bazaar
GREEN LEMONADE

The children of OZ simply love this green lemonade. It is rumoured to be enjoyed by the Wizard himself, with ice and a dash of vodka on a hot day.

YOU WILL NEED

2.5 pints water
2 lemons & 4 limes
6 tablespoon caster sugar, plus extra if you prefer a sweeter drink

✳ Place the water in a deep saucepan. Cut the two lemons and three of the limes in half, squeeze the juice and pips into the water and drop in the squeezed halves. Place over a high heat and bring to the boil (this can take 10 minutes).

✳ Reduce the heat, add the sugar and simmer. Turn off the heat and leave the liquid to cool in the saucepan. As it cools, check the sweetness and add more sugar to taste.

✳ Once cool, strain the lemonade into a jug and chill.

✳ Serve with crushed ice and slices of the reserved lime. For an alcoholic cocktail, add a measure of vodka.

Baum's Bazaar
BAUM'S BUTTONS

These dainty shortbread treats are a cute twist on the basic round cookie.

YOU WILL NEED

200g butter, softened
100g caster sugar
1 teaspoon vanilla extract
200g plain flour
100g ground almonds
Green and blue food colouring

Makes about 50 cookies

To make two different shades of buttons
✶ Divide the ingredients in two before mixing, then colour to different shades.

✶ Place the butter and sugar into a bowl and cream together until light and fluffy. Add a few drops of each food colouring and blend to the desired shade. Add the vanilla extract and mix well.

✶ In a separate bowl, sift the flour and add the ground almonds. Gradually add to the butter to form a dough. Wrap the dough in clingfilm and chill for 2 hours.

✶ Preheat the oven to 160°C/gas mark 3. On a floured surface, roll out the dough to an even thickness of 5mm. Using a 5cm round cookie cutter, press out the button shapes. Place on ungreased baking sheets 1cm apart.

✶ To make the button rim, press a 4cm round jar lid into each cookie. To make the buttonholes, push a cylindrical lolly stick into the centre. Vary the number of holes between four and two. Bake in the oven for 6–10 minutes.

"GREEN CANDY AND GREEN POPCORN WERE OFFERED FOR SALE, AS WELL AS GREEN SHOES, GREEN HATS, AND GREEN CLOTHES OF ALL SORTS. AT ONE PLACE A MAN WAS SELLING GREEN LEMONADE, AND WHEN THE CHILDREN BOUGHT IT DOROTHY COULD SEE THAT THEY PAID FOR IT WITH GREEN PENNIES."

~ Chapter 11 ~
The Wonderful Emerald City of OZ

.1.

PHOTOCOPY THE
CONTAINER ONTO
THIN CARD AND
CUT OUT

.2.

LIGHTLY SCORE
ALONG EACH
FOLD AND GLUE
THE CONTAINER
TOGETHER USING
THE TABS

.3.

FILL THE
CONTAINER WITH
PISTACHIO POPCORN
AND ENJOY

Baum's Bazaar
EMERALD GLASSES

.1.
PHOTOCOPY
THE GLASSES ONTO
THIN CARD AND
CUT OUT

.2.
GLUE THE ARMS TO
THE MAIN FRAME
AND FOLD AT THE
HINGES

.3.
CUT OUT THE
STAR LENSES AND
REPLACE WITH
GREEN SWEET
WRAPPERS

EMERALD
HAIRPIECES

★ ★

These Emerald hairpieces are great for any occasion where you need a little extra sparkle in your life. The different styles are suitable for any hair type, just choose your favourite.

YOU WILL NEED

50cm x 50cm sinamay (use brown for dark hair, beige for fair hair)
1m length of gold cord
A selection of bugle beads, seed beads and any other beads, gems or stones that take your fancy (if the beads have holes then they can be sewn, if they don't then they must be glued)
Appliqué sequin star
Wooden embroidery hoop
Appliqué glue or any other glue that dries clear
Hot glue-gun
Pale coloured thread
Needle
Scissors
Thin metal or fabric-covered hairband
Haircomb

Sinamay is used by milliners in the making of hats and fascinators, so it provides a great base for these emerald hairpieces. Stretching the sinamay over an embroidery hoop keeps it taut and makes it easier to sew the beads in place. If you can't find sinamay, stiff binca for embroidery works just as well. The basic method given here can be used to create either hairpiece designs.

To make the starburst hairpiece
★ Using the template from page 136, trace the starburst shape onto paper and cut out. Mount the sinamay in the embroidery hoop and stretch taut.

fix the template to the sinamay

★ Tape the cutout template to the under side of the sinamay (1).

★ Following the guidelines of the template, lay the gold cord onto the sinamay and secure with small running stitches along the centre. Sew or glue the appliqué sequin star in place. (You can make your own star from sequins, but using an appliqué patch saves time.)

★ Once the cord outline has been completed, gently remove the cutout template from the underside (2). Take care not to rip out any stitches.

★ Starting at the narrow end nearest the star, lay out the largest beads within the cord outline. When you are happy with the design, make a note of the placement of all the beads. Remove the beads and, working one vertical row at at time, begin either sewing or glueing each one in place on the sinamay according to the plan.

attach the hairpiece to a hairband

4

infill the spaces with beads

3

5

✳ Infill the spaces between the larger beads or gems with small bugle or seed beads. It is quicker and neater to thread three or four beads on to thread at a time, then overstitch in place (3).

✳ Once all the spaces have been filled, remove the sinamay from the embroidery hoop and carefully trim away the excess. Coat the reverse side of the design with a thin layer of appliqué glue or any other glue that dries clear; this keeps stray threads in place and strengthens the hairpiece.

✳ Depending on where and how you plan to wear your hairpiece, either hot glue-gun the sinamay onto a hairband or fix in your hair using pins (4).

To make the flower cluster hairpiece
✳ Rather than using a template, this hairpiece was made freehand using teardrop-shaped gems to create each bloom. Stretch the sinamay taut over an embroidery hoop, as before. Using six large teardrop-shape stones, make the centre flower. Sew a sequin in the middle and outline with bugle beads. Using smaller stones, make the two flowers either side and outline with seed beads. Trim the sinamay and coat with a layer of glue, as before. Hot glue-gun the beaded flowers to the upper bar of the haircomb (5).

DECORATED DOGHOUSE

☆ ☆

Spruce up your pooches abode: transform a dull and boring canine kennel into the most desirable doggy digs in the country.

YOU WILL NEED

Wooden dog house, flatpack or pre-made
Sugar soap and sandpaper
Emulsion paint, in chosen colours for base coat and for stencils
3 x A4 sheets of card, for stencils
Thick, dry stencil paintbrush
Fine paintbrush
Matt wood varnish
Gold letters

✴ If you are using a flatpack dog house, assemble it according to the manufacturer's instructions. Wash down all woodwork with sugar soap, then sand down any stray splinters or sharp edges for a smooth paint surface.

✴ Apply a base coat of emulsion to the exterior walls and roof. Allow to dry.

✴ Using the templates from page 136, cut out negative dog shapes in three different sizes and a positive flower shape in one size from the card.

✴ Holding the stencil in position on the walls or roof, dab the emulsion through the card with a stencil paintbrush. Repeat to make the desired pattern. Paint on more detail, such as a scallop edge, with a fine paintbrush.

✴ Once dry, apply a thin coat of wood varnish. Spell out the occupant's name in gold letters above the door.

TOTO'S DOG JACKET

★ ★

Toto truly is a show off, and why not. With a jacket like this your pup will be the most handsome of hounds. The fleece lining makes it the perfect winter coat for any dandy dog

YOU WILL NEED

Tape measure
1m x 1m print fabric
1m x 1m fleece fabric
2m length of 2cm-wide bias binding, in matching colour to print fabric
10cm hook and loop fastening tape
Appliqué sequin stars

★ First, measure up the lucky dog for its new jacket. You need the following measurements: the loose circumference around the widest part of the neck (A); the distance between the nape of the neck and the base of the tail (B); the circumference around the widest part of the chest (C).

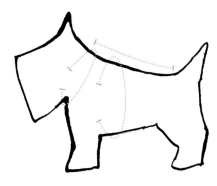

★ Using the template on page 137, scale up the shape to create a bespoke jacket based on your dog's measurements: the curved inner neckline should be the same as measurement A. The length from the neckline to the tail end should be the same as B. The width should be the same as C but less 25cm. Draw up a paper pattern and double-check it by holding it against the dog.

★ Using the paper pattern, cut one jacket shape from both the print and fleece fabrics. With wrong sides facing, place the two jacket pieces together with all raw edges aligning. Pin and tack. Starting at the centre of the lower edge, neaten the outside edge with bias binding, stitching it down by hand or machine. Ease the binding around the curved corners, stretching it gently (1).

★ To make the strap, cut a 30cm x 6cm rectangle from both the print and fleece fabrics. Join, tack and neaten with bias binding as before.

★ Position one end of the strap in the centre of the right-hand side. Pin it to the underside of the jacket, about 5cm from the edge. Work reinforcing stitching over the end by woring a square with a cross inside.

★ Cut a 3cm x 1.5cm piece of fastening tape for the neck and a 5cm x 5cm piece for the waist. Separate the fastening tape into hook pieces and loop pieces. Stitch the separate pieces either side of the neck opening, one on the topside facing upwards and the other on the underside facing downwards. Repeat for the strap with one on the topside of the jacket and one on the underside of the strap (2).

★ Trim with ultra-glam appliqué sequin stars.

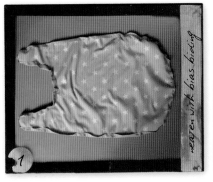

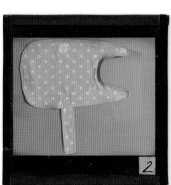

Finest Peanut Butter
TOTO'S TREATS

✶ ✶

Give your own very special dog a treat with Toto's favourite peanut butter cookie snacks.

YOU WILL NEED

200g whole wheat flour
200g plain flour
200ml water
70g peanut butter
2 tablespoons vegetable oil
Bone-shaped cookie cutter

Makes 30–40 treats

✶ Preheat the oven to 175°C/gas mark 4.

✶ In a large bowl, sift together the whole wheat flour and plain flour. Add the water, peanut butter and vegetable oil, then mix well to form a thick dough.

✶ If the dough is too dry, add a few more drops of water to loosen.

✶ On a floured surface, roll out the dough to a thickness of about 5mm. Using a cookie cutter, press out bone shapes. Re-roll all the scraps of dough to make more treats.

✶ Place on ungreased baking sheets. Bake in the oven for 20 minutes. Depending on the size of your oven, bake in batches.

"DOROTHY PUT ON A GREEN SILK APRON AND TIED A GREEN RIBBON AROUND TOTO'S NECK, AND THEY STARTED FOR THE THRONE ROOM OF THE GREAT OZ."

~ Chapter 11 ~
The Wonderful Emerald City of OZ

Roll up! Roll up!
THE GREAT WIZARD'S
THRONE TENT

★ ★

Create your own spectacular tent, one fit for the Great Oz himself! This throne tent is perfect for a child's bedroom or makes extravagant set dressing for a Moroccan-style party.

YOU WILL NEED

3m lengths of 114cm-wide satin fabric in white, emerald and navy
4m of 1cm-wide ribbon, cut into one 20cm length, twelve 10cm lengths and four 65cm lengths
Small plastic hula-hoop, about 60cm in diameter
Lengths of ricrac and pompom trims in various sizes and colours
Appliqué flowers

"DOROTHY FOUND HERSELF IN A WONDERFUL PLACE, A BIG, ROUND ROOM WITH A HIGH ARCHED ROOF, THE WALLS AND CEILING AND FLOOR WERE COVERED WITH LARGE EMERALDS SET CLOSELY TOGETHER."

*~ Chapter 11 ~
The Wonderful City of Oz*

✳ Cut a 50cm piece from each length of satin, shortening them to 2.5m. Set aside the 50cm pieces to use later for the tent roof.

✳ Lay the 2.5m lengths of satin out flat on a clean floor with the longest sides at the top and bottom. Measure and mark the points 32cm down from the top left edge and 32cm up from the bottom right edge. Stretch a piece of string taut across the satin from these two marked points to give a guide for the cutting line (1). Cut the satin along the marked diagonal. You now have six panels.

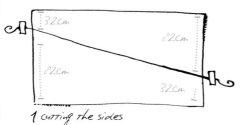

1 cutting the sides

✳ Place the long straight edge of a navy panel together with the long diagonal edge of a white panel, with right sides facing and raw top edges aligned. Stitch with a 1cm seam allowance. As the diagonal edge is longer than the straight edge, an amount of satin will be unstitched at the bottom edge. Repeat for the remaining panels, alternating colours. Turn under and stitch a 1cm hem along the long raw edges of the first and last panels.

✳ Once all the panels are joined, trim away the unstitched excess at the bottom to create a neat curved edge. Turn under and stitch a 1cm hem along this bottom edge.

✳ From each of the 50cm pieces of satin, cut two 30cm equilateral triangles. With right sides facing, join these triangles to form a circle. Stitch with a 1cm seam allowance. Before stitching the final seam, add the hanging loop by folding a 20cm length of ribbon in half and inserting into the seam at the centre of the circle (2). Stitch the seam to complete the circlular tent roof.

✳ Place the roof and main panels together, with right sides facing, aligning the raw edges and matching the seams. Stitch together with 1cm seam allowance.

✳ At each seam junction, secure two 10cm lengths of ribbon to the wrong side with neat handstitches. Turn the tent right side out and place the hula hoop in position where the roof and panels meet. Tie the ribbon pairs into bows to hold the hoop in place.

✳ Attach two 65cm lengths of ribbon to both front panels for tiebacks. Decorate with any embellishments, such as ricrac, pompom trims and readymade appliqué flowers.

THE AMAZING STAR OF OZ

✴ ✴

Bring a little bit of showmanship to any room with this illuminated star.

YOU WILL NEED

A1 sheet of 3mm-thick
foam board
A1 sheet of silver card
Spray mount or PVA glue
Electric drill and drill bit
roughly the same diameter
as the fairylight bulbs
Wooden spoon with
round-ended handle
Metal ruler
Craft knife and cutting mat
String of 20 fairylights with
removable bulbs
Hot-glue gun
Masking tape

*Caution: Do not leave
fairylights unattended when
switched on.*

To make the star

✴ Cut out a 40cm x 40cm square of both foam board and silver card. Spray mount or glue the silver card to the foam board.

✴ Using the template from page 138, trace the star onto the wrong side of the foam board. (From point to point, the star should be 39cm long.) Transfer all the markings.

✴ Using an electric drill, make a hole through the foam board at each of the 20 points marked on the template.

✴ Press the round-ended handle of a wooden spoon into each of the drilled holes to indent the foam board. Press the handle down as firmly as you can (1).

✴ Carefully cut out the star using a metal ruler, craft knife and cutting mat. Apply a little extra glue at each point of the star to make sure the silver card is firmly fixed to the foam board.

✴ Remove each bulb from the string of fairylights. Starting at one point of the star, place the first socket in the hole from the back of the board. Repeat for all 20 sockets (2). Push the bulbs back into the sockets from the silver side through the board. Make sure the holes are large enough or the bulbs and sockets will not properly connect (3).

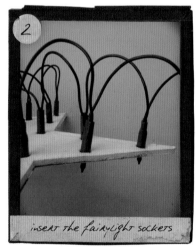

insert the fairylight sockets

fix the sides of the star

For the sides of the star

✳ Cut ten 13cm x 8cm rectangles from the foam board. Working your way around the star, fix one rectangle to each side of the star using a hot glue-gun. For added support, use masking tape to hold the sides in place. At the star point that holds the final light before the plug, leave a gap for the cord to fit through. Don't worry if your rectangles don't join up perfectly as this will be covered up in the next step.

✳ Measure the length each of the sides of your star. They should be 15cm; if not, adjust the length of the rectangle cut in the next step accordingly.

✳ Cut one long 150cm x 8cm rectangle from the silver card. If necessary, this rectangle can be made up of two 75cm x 8cm pieces. Draw a line every 15cm (or the length of the sides of your star)

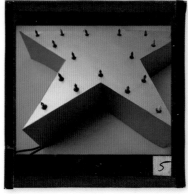

along this rectangle. Score along each of these lines to create a sharp crease.

✳ Apply a thin layer of glue to the card then stick to the sides, neatly butting up to the front edge. The creases will fall into place at the points of the star.

✳ Cut a small hole in the silver card and feed through the electrical cord.

"I AM OZ, THE GREAT AND TERRIBLE. WHO ARE YOU, AND WHY DO YOU SEEK ME?" "I AM DOROTHY, THE SMALL AND MEEK. I HAVE COME TO YOU FOR HELP." "WHAT DO YOU WISH ME TO DO?" "SEND ME BACK TO KANSAS, WHERE MY AUNT EM AND UNCLE HENRY ARE."

"WHY SHOULD I DO THIS FOR YOU?" ASKED OZ. "BECAUSE YOU ARE STRONG AND I AM WEAK; BECAUSE YOU ARE A GREAT WIZARD AND I AM ONLY A LITTLE GIRL."

~ Chapter 11 ~
The Wonderful City of OZ

WHICH WITCH
❧ ARE YOU? ❧

*Answer the following questions to
determine whether you are a more of a
graceful Glinda, than a menacing Mombi.*

1. IF YOU HAD TO LIVE
IN A CERTAIN PART
OF THE COUNTRY
WOULD IT BE...
A: THE EAST OR WEST
B: THE NORTH OR SOUTH

2. WOULD YOU SAY THE
POWER OF GOOD WAS
STRONGER THAN THE
POWER OF EVIL?
A: NO B: YES

3. WHEN YOU LAUGH
DO YOU...
A: HAVE A GOOD CACKLE
B: POLITELY CHIRP,
COVERING YOUR MOUTH
WITH YOUR HAND

4. HOW MANY EYES
DO YOU HAVE?
A: 1 B: 2

5. IF YOU HAD TO HAVE
A PET WOULD IT BE...
A: A MONKEY, IDEALLY
ONE THAT COULD FLY
B: I DON'T HAVE PETS,
AS I AM TOO DELICATE
AND ALLERGIC

6. ON A FUN NIGHT
OUT WOULD YOU
PREFER TO...
A: COMMAND YOUR
MONKEY ARMY
TO DESTROY ALL
TRESPASSERS ON
YOUR LAND
B: FLOAT AROUND IN A
BUBBLE OF LOVLINESS

7. WHEN SHAPING
YOUR NAILS, DO
YOU FIND THAT...
A: YOU NEED TO CLIP
THEM WITH GARDEN
SHEARS, AS THEY ARE
SO TOUGH
B: BUFFING WITH A
SIMPLE NAIL FILE
WILL SUFFICE

8. YOUR FAVOURITE
DRESS IS...
A: DEFINETLY THE
BLACK ONE WITH THE
HIGH COLLAR AND
MATCHING CAPE
B: I CAN'T DECIDE,
THERE ARE SO MANY,
OH, I DON'T KNOW...
SOMETHING PINK

RESULTS

MOSTLY As
My, oh, my. You are a
dastardly witch, through
and through. You have
a very devious streak and
a taste for the alternative.
Your tattered clothes,
threatening nature,
struggle for power and
cackle give you away
as a person to avoid.

MOSTLY Bs
What a goodie-two-shoes
you are. A delicate and
pretty thing who scares
easily, you love to sing
and dance – sometimes to
the annoyance of others.
Looking in the mirror
is one of your favourite
pastimes, because you
are just so perfect.

**EVEN NUMBER
OF As & Bs**
You are the perfect mix
of good and bad; the
best way to be. You
have the beauty of a
good witch with the
sassiness and bad-ass
attitude of a bad witch.

I'm melting!
WITCH CANDLES

✮ ✮

Use a cookie cutter to make these ingenious candles and watch your wicked witch disappear in a puff of smoke. These candles look great flying together in a coven.

YOU WILL NEED

Paraffin wax pellets or beads
Tin can or metal jug
Old saucepan
Black candle dye in chips or pellets
Medium lead free wire wick
Plastic jug
Baking tray with sides
Baking parchment
Witch-shaped cookie cutter
Black table candles
Wooden toothpicks

✴ Place the wax pellets or beads in a tin can or metal jug. Place the tin can in an old saucepan, if ncessary resting on a trivet. Fill the saucepan with cold water to just below the rim of the can or jug. Bring the water to the boil, then turn the heat down to a simmer until the wax melts. When the wax is molten, add some black candle dye.

✴ Line the baking tray with parchment. Pour the black wax into the lined tray, leaving a small amount in the can or jug. Allow the wax to cool until it is pliable and soft to the touch.

✴ Using the cookie cutter, press out two witch shapes per candle and peel away from the parchment. Place a length of wick on the inside of one wax shape, starting at the bottom of the witch and extending beyond the top of her hat. Lay a wooden toothpick on the bottom third of the wax shape (1).

✴ Using the leftover wax, stick the second wax witch shape on top of the first, matching

insert the wick & toothpick

up the contours and sandwiching the wick and toothpick in between. Allow to cool.

✴ Cut the tops of the black table candles and place in a microwave for 10 seconds to soften the wax.

✴ Make a hole in the top of each table candle by skewering with a toothpick. Position the witch-shaped candles in the tops of the table candles by slotting the toothpick into the hole.

"SHE PICKED UP THE BUCKET OF WATER THAT STOOD NEAR AND DASHED IT OVER THE WITCH, WETTING HER FROM HEAD TO FOOT...INSTANTLY THE WICKED WOMAN GAVE A LOUD CRY OF FEAR, AND THEN, AS DOROTHY LOOKED AT HER IN WONDER, THE WITCH BEGAN TO SHRINK AND FALL AWAY.

~ Chapter 12 ~
The Search for the Wicked Witch

"We will carry you," replied the King, and no sooner had he spoken than two of the Monkeys caught Dorothy in their arms and flew away with her. Others took the Scarecrow and the Woodman and the Lion, and one little Monkey seized Toto and flew after them, although the dog tried hard to bite him.

~ Chapter 14 ~
The Winged Monkeys

PARTY

PARTEI

Soirée

Winged Monkey

PARTY INVITES

★ ★

Send your very own troop of winged monkeys to deliver news of your fabulous party!

YOU WILL NEED

For each invite:
A4 sheet of patterned
scrapbook card
A4 sheet of silver card
12cm x 10cm thick white
card
Rubber alphabet stamps

★ Using the templates on page 138, cut out one body from each patterned scrapbook card and two wings for each body from silver card.

★ Crease each wing along the dotted line marked on the template. Glue the wings to the body where indicated on the template.

★ Fold the white card in half lengthways. On the front of the card, print your party message using the rubber stamps. Write any further details inside the card by hand. Glue the card to the hands of your monkey.

Little Monkey's BABIES BATH TOWEL

*This cuddly bath towel is just right for all the little monkeys out there.
For a newborn baby cut a 50cm square from the towel and adjust the
size of all the other pieces accordingly.*

YOU WILL NEED

Brown bath towel
2.7m bias binding or velvet ribbon,
about 2cm wide
Beige hand towel
50cm x 50cm yellow cotton fabric
Two 3cm circles black felt for eyes
Matching sewing threads
Brown and pink embroidery thread
50cm x 40cm polyester wadding
Red wool pompom
Appliqué sequin stars

✴ Cut a 75cm x 75cm square from the
brown bath towel. At three points of
the square, round off the corners to a
gentle curve.

✴ Starting and stopping about 20cm
along from the square corner, neaten
the outside edge with bias binding,
stitching it down by hand or machine.
Ease the bind around the curved
corners, stretching it gently (1). If you
are using velvet ribbon, fold it in half
lengthways first and press.

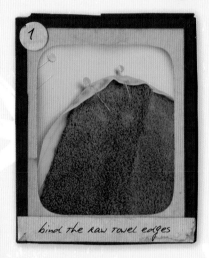

bind the raw towel edges

To make the monkey's face
✴ Cut a 44cm x 30cm x 30cm triangle from
the brown hand towel. If possible, use the
natural selvedge of the towel as the longest
straight side of the triangle. If this isn't
possible, hem the edge to prevent fraying.

✴ Using the template from page 139, cut one
muzzle from the beige flannel. Embroider
onto the muzzle a wide mouth in brown
thread with chain stitch and two small
nostrils in pink thread with straight stitch.
With the longest edge of the triangle at the
bottom, position the muzzle to create the
monkey's face. Pin and stitch in place. Sew
in place the two black felt circles for eyes.

✴ Using the template on page 139,
cut two inner ears from yellow cotton.

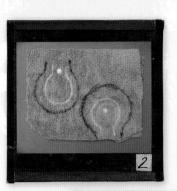

Place right sides up on a scrap of brown towel 10cm apart. Zigzag stitch around the edges. Using the outer ear template, trace the outlines on to the wrong side of the towel, with a 2cm margin all the way round the stitch lines (2).

✶ Place this scrap of towel together with a second piece, with right sides facing. Stitch around the outlines, leaving a turning hole at the base of each ear. Trim the excess fabric close to the lines of stitching. Turn right sides out. Pinch the base of the ears together and secure with a few hand stitches (3).

✶ Lay out the large square of brown towel with the unbound square corner at the top. Position the ears at the top, one on each side about 10cm down from the corner facing into the square. Place the monkey's face on top, with right sides facing and aligning the raw edges (4). Machine stitch making a curve at the corner. If your machine cannot stitch through all the layers at the ears, leave that section unstitched and then sew it by hand. Zigzag stitch all the raw edges to prevent fraying and trim any excess fabric. Turn right side out. The ears will pop into place.

For the monkey's wings
✶ Pin together 50cm x 40cm pieces of beige towel and yellow cotton with right sides facing. Using the wing template on page 139, trace one outline on to the wrong side of the cotton. Flip the template over and trace a second outline. Stitch, leaving turning holes where marked on the template. Trim the excess fabric close to the lines of stitching. Turn right sides out.

✶ Using the same template, cut out two wing-shaped pieces of wadding. Feed the wadding into the sewn wings, trimming if necessary for a good fit (5).

✶ To quilt the wings, topstitch along the dotted lines marked on the template.

✶ Neatly close the opening on each wing with small neat hand stitches. Stitch the wings in place on the back of the towel, 25cm down from the hood.

✶ Decorate with a red pompom on the point of the hood and appliqué sequin stars on the front edges.

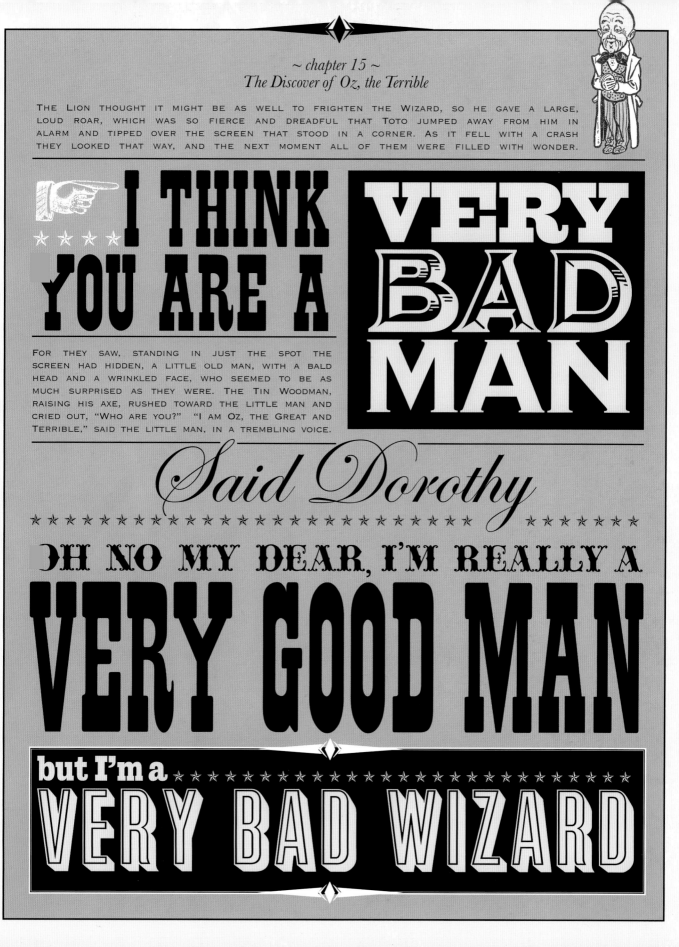

THE LION THOUGHT IT MIGHT BE AS WELL TO FRIGHTEN THE WIZARD, SO HE GAVE A LARGE, LOUD ROAR, WHICH WAS SO FIERCE AND DREADFUL THAT TOTO JUMPED AWAY FROM HIM IN ALARM AND TIPPED OVER THE SCREEN THAT STOOD IN A CORNER. AS IT FELL WITH A CRASH THEY LOOKED THAT WAY, AND THE NEXT MOMENT ALL OF THEM WERE FILLED WITH WONDER.

...I THINK YOU ARE A

VERY BAD MAN

FOR THEY SAW, STANDING IN JUST THE SPOT THE SCREEN HAD HIDDEN, A LITTLE OLD MAN, WITH A BALD HEAD AND A WRINKLED FACE, WHO SEEMED TO BE AS MUCH SURPRISED AS THEY WERE. THE TIN WOODMAN, RAISING HIS AXE, RUSHED TOWARD THE LITTLE MAN AND CRIED OUT, "WHO ARE YOU?" "I AM OZ, THE GREAT AND TERRIBLE," SAID THE LITTLE MAN, IN A TREMBLING VOICE.

Said Dorothy

* *

OH NO MY DEAR, I'M REALLY A

VERY GOOD MAN

but I'm a *

VERY BAD WIZARD

THE SCARECROW.
"IF MY HEAD STAYS STUFFED
WITH STRAW INSTEAD OF
BRAINS... HOW AM I TO
EVER KNOW ANYTHING?"

DOROTHY
"I AM ANXIOUS TO GET BACK
TO MY AUNT AND UNCLE,
FOR I AM SURE THEY WILL
WORRY ABOUT ME. CAN YOU
HELP ME FIND MY WAY?"

Oz Apothecary
SLEEPY-TIME SALT SCRUB WITH LAVENDER

YOU WILL NEED

120g coarse sea salt
4 heads dried
lavender flowers
5 drops lavender
essence
50ml olive oil
Storage jar

Skin type: all

✴ Place all the ingredients together in a large bowl and mix thoroughly.

✴ Transfer to a storage jar with a tight seal, such as a Kilner jar. This scrub can be kept for up to two weeks.

How to use
✴ When bathing or showering, rub a handful of the scrub over your body to exfoliate any dead skin. Your skin will be left feeling ultra-moisturised and soft.

Oz Apothecary
FACE MASK OF ETERNAL YOUTH

The banana is the secret to this oatmeal and honey face mask; a rich source of vitamins, an anti-inflammatory and stuffed with antioxidants, it gives skin a supple youthful glow.

YOU WILL NEED

1 medium banana
1 teaspoon honey
¼ teaspoon jojoba oil
100g rolled oats

Skin type: all

✴ Place the banana and the honey in a bowl. Mash together to form a paste. Add the jojoba oil. Stir in the oats.

How to use
✴ Apply liberally to a fully cleansed face, avoiding the eye area. Leave for 15 minutes. Rinse off with warm water. Your skin with be left rejuvenated and glowing.

❦ "PUT A BRAVE FACE ON IT" ❧
SKIN TONIC

Not only does this delightfully aromatic tonic tone, it also calms and hydrates,
leaving your skin feeling ready to face the world once again.

YOU WILL NEED

20 fragrant rose heads
4 pints water
Bag of ice cubes
Two small heatproof bowls
Large metal saucepan with lid

Skin type: normal – dry

✶ Separate the petals from the rose heads, discarding any stems and leaves. Rinse thoroughly in cold water.

✶ Place a small heatproof bowl upside down in the centre of the saucepan. Scatter the rose petals around the bowl inside the saucepan. On top of the upside-down bowl, rest a second bowl the right way up.

✶ Pour enough water into the saucepan to just cover the rose petals. Do not pour any water into the bowls. Place the lid on the saucepan, but upside down.

✶ Turn on the heat and bring the water to the boil. Once boiling, reduce to a low heat and simmer for 5 minutes.

✶ Fill the inverted saucepan lid with ice cubes. The rosewater will collect in the bowl inside the saucepan: check every 10 minutes to see how much rosewater has collected. Replenish the melted ice. Stop this process once you have collected about 1 pint of rosewater. The entire process should take about 30 minutes.

✶ Transfer to a sterile container and allow to cool. This tonic can be kept for up to two weeks.

How to use
✶ To use as a toner, apply to the face after cleansing. Dab onto a cotton wool pad and gently wipe over the skin. This helps to refine pours, reduce puffiness and moisturise.

✶ Rosewater can also be used as a make-up remover, an aftershave, to treat sunburn, to reduce swelling, to soothe a headache and even in cooking.

The Wonderful Wizard's
BALLOON MOBILE

✯ ✯

The wonderful Wizard escaped OZ in a hot-air balloon made from different pieces of green silk. These paper balloons waft gently in the breeze and are mesmerising in a child's room.

YOU WILL NEED

Various sheets of plain and patterned scrapbook paper: for the largest balloon, you will need enough sheets to cut thirty 26cm diameter circles. (The balloons work best if the paper is all of a similar thickness.)
Craft knife or pair of scissors
Pinking shears
Double-sided adhesive tape
Hot glue-gun or superglue
Coloured or metallic embroidery thread
Gems, buttons or paper shapes for extra decoration
Bradawl and cutting mat
Strong thread, such as button or bookbinding
Large needle
Invisible fishing wire

These paper balloons look beautiful swaying in the breeze and provide an unusual focal point, either placed above a bed or hung in a group over a dining table. The following instructions are for the large green balloon shown in the photograph opposite. Enlarge or reduce the size of the circles and the basket to make larger or smaller balloons.

To make the basket
✯ For the basket base, draw an 8.5cm diameter circle onto a sheet of paper and cut out with an extra 1cm all the way round. Score around the drawn circle with the blunt edge of a craft knife or pair of scissors. Make small snips into the outer 1cm, about 5mm apart, around the circumference of the circle to make little tabs. Fold these tabs upwards. For the basket sides, cut a 30cm x 6cm rectangle from the same paper. For a decorative edge, use pinking shears.

make the basket

1

✯ Place double-sided adhesive tape along one long and one short edge of the rectangle. Peel off the backing papers. Join the sides to the base by fixing the rectangle to the cut tabs of the circle, pressing down each tab. Once attached to the base, press the short edges of the sides together to secure (1).

To make the swags
✯ Using the template on page 139, trace the outline onto paper four times. Score along the middle line marked on the template.

2

Gently pinch each swag to make it 3D (2).

✯ Using a hot glue-gun, fix the swags evenly round the basket so they just touch, about 1cm down from the top edge. At the point where two swags meet, glue a 20cm length of embroidery thread. Cover the join with a decorative gem, button or paper shape.

To make the balloon
✯ Cut out thirty to forty 26cm diameter circles from various coloured and patterned papers. The more circles you use, the fuller

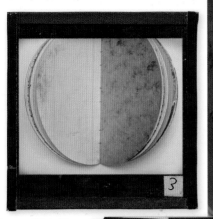

decorate the basket

the balloon will be. For smaller balloons, use fewer paper circles.

✳ Fold each circle in half. Make two equal stacks of semi circles. Place the two stacks next to each other to form a whole circle.

✳ For the stitching guide, measure and mark the points 4cm down from the top edge and 4cm up from the bottom edge of each semi circle. Make another mark 2cm further in. Repeat at the middle. For the hanging loop, using a bradawl make a hole 1cm down from the top edge of each stack of circles.

✳ Take one of the stacks and open out the circles so they lay flat. Using a

bradawl and a cutting mat, make holes at each mark through all the circles of paper. Using strong thread and a large needle, stitch the circles together. Repeat for the second stack of circles. Place one sewn stack on top of the other and stitch together to make one big stack. Make sure the first half of the circles bend one way, then the second half bend the other way.

✳ Run a length of invisible fishing wire through the top hole. Suspend your balloon at a height where it is easy to work with. The paper leaves will naturally fan out to create a sphere.

✳ Fix the basket to the balloon by stitching through a different paper

leave for each string. Spend time finding the right leaves so the basket hangs straight. You can temporarily fix the basket strings in place with glue dots whilst experimenting with different position.

✳ Using the template on page 139, cut out bows from paper for the kite tails. Concertina the centre of each bow and fix with a few hand stitches.

✳ Add kite tails to the basket, decorated with strings of paper bows. or small triangles to make bunting.

"COME, DOROTHY!" CRIED THE WIZARD, "HURRY UP, OR THE BALLOON WILL FLY AWAY."

"I CAN'T FIND TOTO ANYWHERE," REPLIED DOROTHY, WHO DID NOT WISH TO LEAVE HER LITTLE DOG BEHIND.

~ Chapter 17 ~
How the Balloon was Launched

DRESS-UP DOROTHY & TOTO

enlarge by 200%

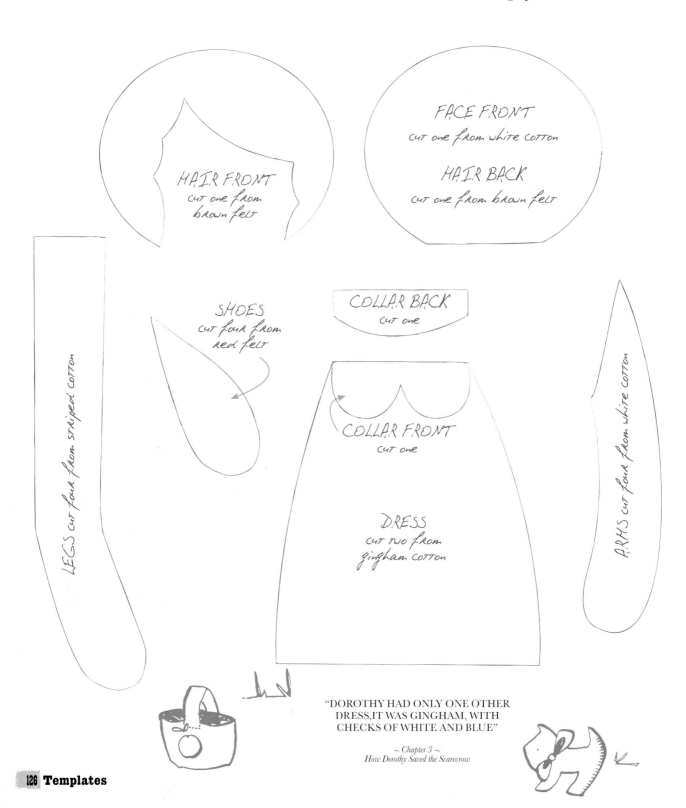

HAIR FRONT
cut one from
brown felt

FACE FRONT
cut one from white cotton

HAIR BACK
cut one from brown felt

SHOES
cut four from
red felt

COLLAR BACK
cut one

COLLAR FRONT
cut one

DRESS
cut two from
gingham cotton

LEGS cut four from striped cotton

ARMS cut four from white cotton

"DOROTHY HAD ONLY ONE OTHER
DRESS, IT WAS GINGHAM, WITH
CHECKS OF WHITE AND BLUE"

~ Chapter 3 ~
How Dorothy Saved the Scarecrow

LION HEAD
CUT TWO FROM YELLOW FELT

LION EAR
CUT TWO

LION MANE
CUT ONE FROM
ORANGE FELT

LION
MUZZLE
CUT ONE FROM
CREAM FELT

APRON
CUT ONE FROM
GINGHAM COTTON

TOTO
CUT TWO FROM
BLACK FELT

APRON POCKET
CUT ONE

BASKET SIDES
CUT TWO FROM
BROWN FELT

TOTO CUSHION

★ ★

enlarge by 300%

"COME ALONG, TOTO,' SHE SAID.
'WE SHALL GO TO THE EMERALD CITY
AND ASK THE GREAT OZ HOW TO GET
BACK TO KANSAS"

~ Chapter 3 ~
How Dorothy Saved the Scarecrow

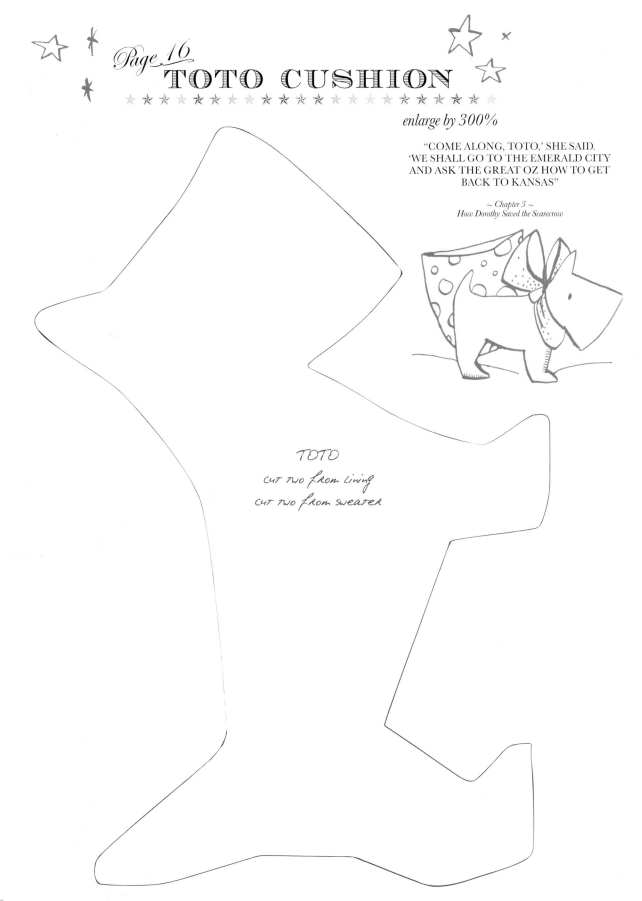

TOTO

CUT TWO FROM LINING

CUT TWO FROM SWEATER

Page 36

MUNCHKIN HAT EGG COSIES

✦ ✦

enlarge egg cosy by 120%   *enlarge accessories by 200%*

HAT
CUT ONE

BRIM
CUT ONE

FLOWER PETALS CUT TWO

FLOWER CENTRE
CUT ONE

FEATHER

Page 38

MUNCHKIN PLACECARDS

✦ ✦ ✦ ✦ ✦ ✦ ✦ ✦ ✦ ✦ ✦ ✦ ✦ ✦ ✦ ✦ ✦ ✦ ✦

enlarge by 200%

GIRL
FACE

BOY
FACE

APRON

Page 34

GLINDA PEG DOLL

✦ ✦ ✦ ✦ ✦ ✦ ✦ ✦ ✦ ✦ ✦ ✦ ✦

copy at 100%

enlarge in relation to your scarecrow sticks

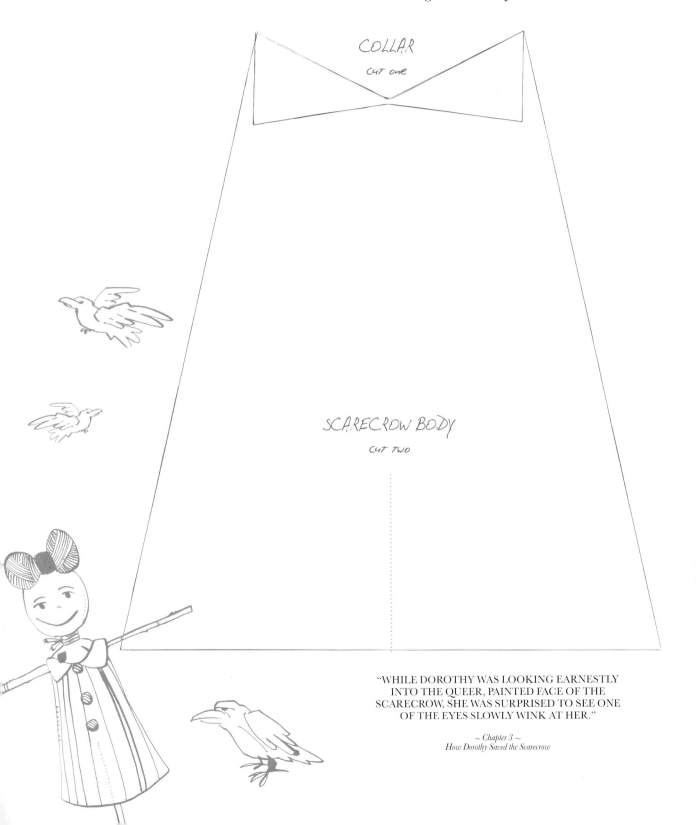

COLLAR

CUT ONE

SCARECROW BODY

CUT TWO

"WHILE DOROTHY WAS LOOKING EARNESTLY
INTO THE QUEER, PAINTED FACE OF THE
SCARECROW, SHE WAS SURPRISED TO SEE ONE
OF THE EYES SLOWLY WINK AT HER."

~ Chapter 3 ~
How Dorothy Saved the Scarecrow

copy at 100%

BIRD WING
cut two

HEART
cut as many
in each size
as you prefer

BIRD
cut two

COWARDLY LION HAND PUPPET

★ ★

enlarge by 150%

A

BACK
cut one from yellow felt

FRONT
cut one from yellow felt

EARS
cut two from orange felt

NOSE
cut one from pink felt

FACE
cut one from yellow felt

C

INNER EARS
cut two from pink felt

B

MOUTH
cut one from pink felt

fold line

MUZZLE
cut one from cream felt

C

B

A

"THAT DOESN'T MAKE ME ANY BRAVER, AND AS LONG AS I KNOW MYSELF TO BE A COWARD I SHALL BE UNHAPPY."

~ Chapter 6 ~
The Cowardly Lion

TUMMY
cut one from print fabric

PAW
cut two from various

ARM
cut four from yellow felt

FIELD-O-POPPIES

✦ ✦

enlarge by 225%

POPPY PETAL

"THEY NOW CAME UPON
MORE AND MORE OF THE
BIG SCARLET POPPIES,
AND FEWER OF THE
OTHER FLOWERS.

~ Chapter 8 ~
The Deadly Poppy Field

POPPY STAMEN

SLEEPY-TIME EYEMASK

enlarge by 110%

EYEMASK
cut two from silk and cut one from soft velor (lining fabric)

A   B

EMBROIDERY GUIDE

● Running Stitch   ● Straight Stitch   ● Split Stitch   ● French knot

Divide the thread of the preceding stitch with the needle when entering material

EMERALD HAIRPIECES

copy at 100%

Page 94

PATCHWORK SITTERS

enlarge by 300%

Page 76

Page 96
TOTO'S DOG HOUSE
✴ ✴ ✴ ✴ ✴ ✴ ✴ ✴ ✴ ✴ ✴ ✴ ✴ ✴ ✴ ✴ ✴ ✴ ✴

scale to suit your dog house

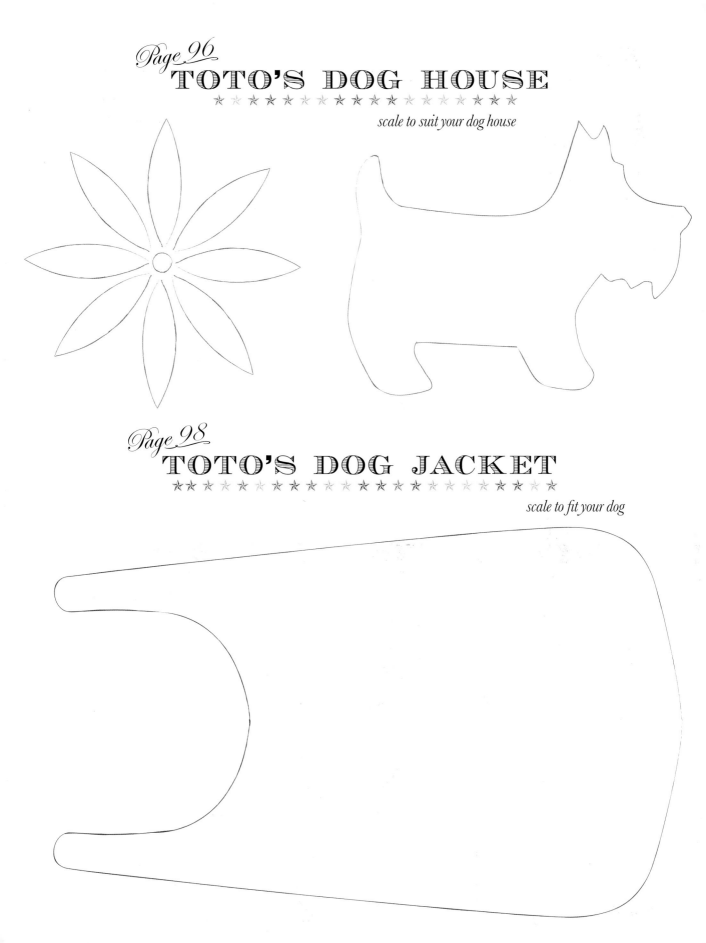

Page 98
TOTO'S DOG JACKET
✴ ✴

scale to fit your dog

Page 104
STAR OF OZ
★ ★ ★ ★ ★ ★ ★ ★ ★ ★ ★ ★ ★ ★ ★ ★ ★ ★ ★

enlarge by 400%

STAR
cut one from
foam board and
silver card

Page 110
WINGED MONKEY INVITES
★ ★

enlarge by 200%

MONKEY WING
cut two from silver card

MONKEY BODY
cut one from
patterned paper

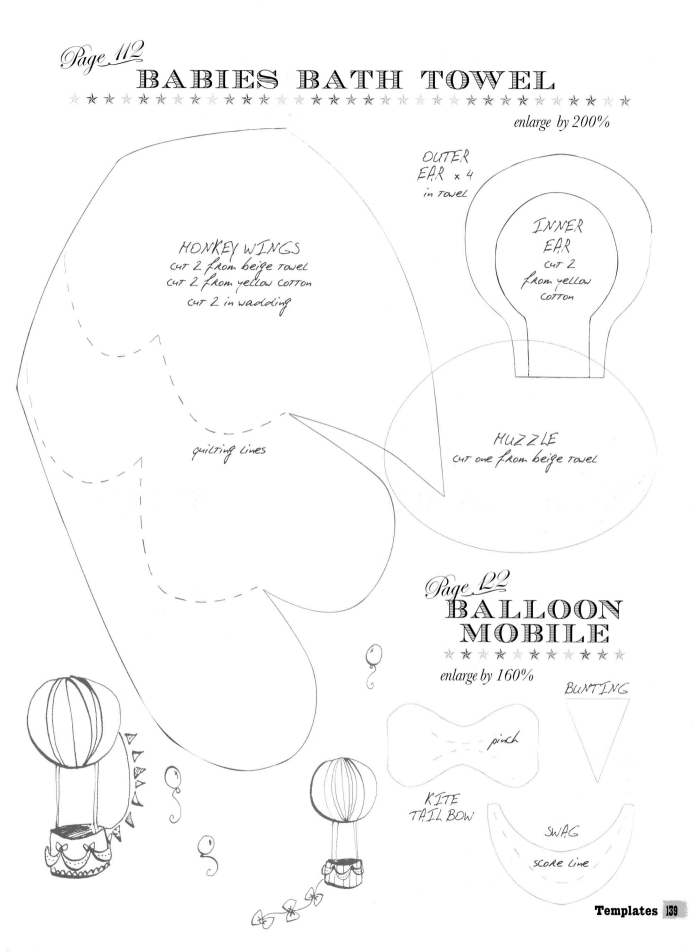

Page 112

BABIES BATH TOWEL

✻ ✻

enlarge by 200%

OUTER
EAR x 4
in towel

INNER
EAR
cut 2
from yellow
cotton

MONKEY WINGS
cut 2 from beige towel
cut 2 from yellow cotton
cut 2 in wadding

quilting lines

MUZZLE
cut one from beige towel

Page 22

BALLOON
MOBILE

✻ ✻ ✻ ✻ ✻ ✻ ✻ ✻ ✻ ✻ ✻ ✻

enlarge by 160%

BUNTING

pinch

KITE
TAIL BOW

SWAG

score line

DIRECTORY

*While making the projects in this book, we found many inspiring places
for supplies and ideas. Here are some of our favourites.*

SUPPLIERS

Always Hobbies

*An excellent online resource of
hobby materials, everything from
aluminium sheets to dolls house
supplies and tools.*
01508 549 330
www.alwayshobbies.com

Barnett Lawson

*Behind a plain door and down
a set of stairs is this amazing
unexpected treasure trove of buttons
and other trimmings.*
16–17 Little Portland Street
London W1W 8NE
020 7636 8591
www.bltrimmings.com

The Bead Shop Manchester

*One of the best jewellery making
resources you can find online.*
18 Upper Chorlton Road
Manchester M16 7RN
0161 232 7356
www.the-beadshop.co.uk

Blade Rubber

*Supplier of lovely rubber stamps
and inks plus other crafty things.*
12 Bury Place
London WC1A 2JL
020 7831 4123
www.bladerubberstamps.co.uk

Blooming Felt

*A one-stop shop for all your felt needs,
including craft sheets and shapes.*
Howe Green Farm
Southend Road
Howe Green CM2 7TW
01245 471 690
www.bloomingfelt.co.uk

The Cloth House

47 & 98 Berwick Street
London W1F 0QJ
020 7437 5155
020 7287 1555
www.clothhouse.com

The Dover Book Shop

*Royalty-free vintage illustrations
and typefaces for your craft projects.*
18 Earlham Street
London WC2H 9LG
020 7836 2111
www.doverbooks.co.uk

eBay

*A brilliant way to snap up
bargains on vintage china.
Remember to look for pretty brands
such as Shelly, Tuscan China,
Foley and Wedgwood.*
www.ebay.com

Fabric Rehab

*Lovely supplier of fabrics for
patchwork and other projects.
Lots of cute Japanese designs.*
www.fabricrehab.co.uk

HobbyCraft

*The perfect place for general craft
and cookery supplies. Check the
website for your local store.*
01202 596100
www.hobbycraft.co.uk

Jack Straws Country Store

*A huge selection of reasonably priced
straw baskets, perfect for Dorothy.*
6 Santa Maria Way
Stourport on Severn
Worcs DY13 9RX
07917 005619
www.jackstrawscountry
store.co.uk

Klein's

An Aladdin's cave of fantastic trims; take the time to have a good rummage.
5 Noel Street
London W1F 8GD
020 7437 6162
www.kleins.co.uk

Lakeland Plastics

Great for specialist items such as unusual cake moulds and edible glitter. Check the website for your local store.
01539 488 100
www.lakeland.co.uk

Liberty

An oasis of calm just five minutes from the hustle and bustle of Oxford Street.
Great Marlborough Street
London W1B 5AH
020 7734 1234
www.liberty.co.uk

London Graphic Centre

Supplier of a huge range of general art and graphic supplies.
16–18 Shelton Street
London WC2H 9JL
020 7759 4500
www.londongraphics.co.uk

MacCulloch & Wallis

Just off Oxford street this store is a great place to get fine fabrics, millinery goods and trims.
25–26 Dering Street
London W1S 1AT
020 7629 0311
www.macculloch-wallis.co.uk

Myriad Natural Toys

A great selection of 100% wool felt in a myriad of colours.
01725 517 085
www.myriadonline.co.uk

"I HAVE COME FOR MY COURAGE," ANNOUNCED THE LION, ENTERING THE ROOM."

~ Chapter 16 ~
The Magic Art of the GreatHumbug

Paperchase

The flagship store has a whole floor of craft papers, cards and supplies.
12 Alfred Place
London WC1E 7EB
020 7467 6200
www.paperchase.co.uk

Squires Kitchen Sugarcraft

Online shop boasting a massive range of cake decorating goodies.
0845 617 1810
www.squires-shop.com

The Trimming Company

Wonderful online resource for sinamay and hat-making supplies.
www.thetrimmingcompany.com

V.V. Rouleaux

An inspirational store crammed full of beautiful ribbons and trims.
49 Hallam Street
London W1U 2QD
020 7224 5179
www.vvrouleaux.com

INSPIRATION

MUSEUMS

If you are a die-hard OZ fan, why not hop on a flight to the United States and visit Kansas, the hometown of the book.

The OZ Museum

In the heart of Kansas, this museum is the place to go for all OZ fans.
511 Lincoln
Wamego
Kansas 66547
1-866-458-TOTO
www.ozmuseum.com

Land of Oz

An Oz-based theme park that is available for both party hire and small private tours.
Beech Mountain Parkway
Beech Mountain
North Carolina 28604
1-828-387-2000
www.emeraldmtn.com

THEATRE & FILM

Why not get inspired and have a good old-fashioned singalong by seeing these fantastic adaptations of the OZ story.

The Wizard of OZ

(1939, MGM) How many of us first heard of the Wizard of OZ tale, this film is a timeless classic starring Judy Garland.

Wizard of OZ

Based on the MGM film adaptation, this musical is great fun for all the family.
London Palladium
Argyll Street
London W1F 7TF
0844 412 4655
www.wizardofozthemusical.com

Wicked

This musical tells the witches' story before we meet them in the book. Filled with fantastic original songs, it is well worth seeing.
Apollo Victoria
Wilton Road
London SW1V 1LG
0844 544 3830
www.wickedthemusical.co.uk

BLOGS

everythingozbook.blogspot.com
theozenthusiast.blogspot.com
thewizardofozblog.com
ozmapolitan.wordpress.com

Christine is blogging at
sewyeah.co.uk
and Hannah at
couturecraft.blogspot.co.uk

WITH THANKS

*Our sincerest thanks to L. Frank Baum for writing **The Wizard of OZ**. To Mr & Mrs Peters for their kindness in sharing their farm with us. To Verity the Chicken Catcher. To Lisa, Nikki, James, Jane, Alison and all at Quadrille Publishing for their continuing support. To Jan at HobbyCraft Plc for kindly sponsoring the fabric used in this book.*

Christine *Thank you again to everyone for their support during the making of the book, especially to Mum and Dad with their location scouting and kindly opening their house to us. To Aunty and Uncle for their advice on everything… To Nanny and Grandad for just being them. To Jo, Ian, Oliver & Elliot. To Joe and Joel and all the other Buzzers, fun times. To Jake, Kirsty and Laura for keeping me sane. Love you all.*

Hannah *My darling Brendan, thank you for once again putting up with all my crafty behaviour in our home. To Mum & Dad for taking me repeatedly to see our friend Charlie in The Wizard of OZ as a child. To Charlie Drake for gifting me his favourite book, Down the Yellow Brick Road by Doug McClelland. A big thank you to both Antonia – mummy to Maggie, our Toto – as well as Anna & James – parents of Christian, our flying monkey – for letting them model for us!*